Christmas is Coming!
1988

Compiled and Edited
by Linda Martin Stewart

© 1988 by Oxmoor House, Inc.
Book Division of Southern Progress Corporation
P.O. Box 2463, Birmingham, Alabama 35201

Library of Congress Catalog Card Number:
84-63030

ISBN: 0-8487-0721-4
ISSN: 0883-9077

Manufactured in the United States of America
First Printing

Executive Editor: Candace N. Conard
Production Manager: Jerry Higdon
Associate Production Manager: Rick Litton
Art Director: Bob Nance

Christmas Is Coming! 1988

Editor: Linda Martin Stewart
Illustrator and Designer: Barbara Ball
Editorial Assistant: Jennifer M. Zanon
Production Assistant: Theresa L. Beste
Copy Chief: Mary Jean Haddin
Photographer: Colleen Duffley
Photo Stylist: Connie Formby

To find out how you can order *Cooking Light*
magazine, write to *Cooking Light*®, P.O. Box
C-549, Birmingham, AL 35283

Contents

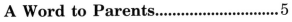

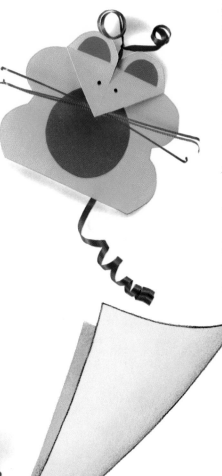

Parents' Workshop: Great Gifts for Children

A Word to Parents

In its fourth year, *CHRISTMAS IS COMING!* is again packed with the pick of holiday projects. And I continue to be amazed at the creative talent that lies behind them. Many of you have asked where the ideas come from. Do I think them up? Do I sew and stencil and saw and knit? Only in my dreams!

In reality, I have a growing list of designers who supply *CHRISTMAS IS COMING!* with its wealth of craft and gift ideas. The variety and quality of the projects they submit are remarkable. In addition, these people are adaptable and dependable—a genuine pleasure to work with. You'll find their names on the last page of this book. Please give them a round of mental applause!

Featuring holiday affairs for pint-sized party goers, COME ONE, COME ALL is the first chapter in *CHRISTMAS IS COMING! 1988.* Within these pages, youngsters will find a trio of parties planned with them in mind. (No fussy clothes and no funny foods.) Kids will have a ball crooning Christmas tunes, while dressed as stars, reindeer, and other symbols of the season. For some good, gooey fun, they can prepare a meal for the birds. Or they can don Santa hats and beards and hold a workshop—fashion Christmas crafts and dine on Santa-sack lunches.

More fun for youngsters is theirs for the making in CHILDREN'S WORKSHOP. Dip-and-drape angels, soapbox soldiers, and grocery-sack stockings are just a few of the Christmas trimmings to fix. As for presents to make, there's a car wash kit for Dad, froggie banks for friends, and tub-time stick-um ups for baby brothers and sisters.

As always, color photographs and illustrations, full-size patterns, and numbered instructions are included with each of the projects in CHILDREN'S WORKSHOP. As you glance over these projects, notice that suggestions (Before you start) or words of caution (For safety's sake) occasionally precede the instructions.

Note also that at the bottom of the first page of each project, there is a level rating of 1, 2, or 3, with Level 1 indicating the quickest, easiest projects, and Level 3 the most difficult ones or those calling for adult supervision. The projects within Level 2 are simple but call for a certain skill, such as measuring, or for extra time and patience. Please understand that these ratings are intended only as a guide. You best know your children's capabilites. Look through the projects and decide together which ones are suitable for them to make.

A grab bag of children's gifts awaits grown-ups in PARENTS' WORKSHOP. Outfit kids from head to toe with projects from "Grin and Wear It," or turn to "Suite Dreams" and select a special gift for a bedroom. "Just for Fun" presents the perfect toddler toy, a holiday folder, a honey of a purse, a necklace, and a prize pair—TuTu and Tango, the dancing dolls.

With these craft and gift ideas, your family will be as busy as Santa's this season. May Christmas 1988 be the merriest ever—full of joy, peace, and lots of love!

Linda Martin Stewart

Come One, Come All!

Christmas Parties for Kids

Costume Caroling Party

Christmas is coming! Soon you'll be busy baking cookies, making a wish list, trimming the tree, and wrapping presents. School will be out for the holidays. (Yea!) Like magic, excitement will fill the air, and familiar symbols of the season—wreaths, manger scenes, lighted trees—will appear everywhere. How happy you are, and what fun it is to share your good feelings with others!

A caroling party is a super way to share those feelings. This Christmas, why not round up the children in your neighborhood and ask them to come. Set a date and a time for the party. Plan to sing door-to-door on your street, or have your mom make arrangements for you to go and cheer up kids in the hospital.

8

To make the party extra merry, tell the carolers to dress as their favorite holiday characters. Some cute costumes are pictured here. We used foam core to make the star, tree ornaments, antlers, gift box, and angel wings. Santa is wearing a sweatsuit trimmed with cotton batting. See how many other Christmas characters you and your buddies can think of.

Several days before the party, ask a grown-up to make copies of your favorite carols, so you can assemble songbooks. When your group gathers, hand out the books and practice singing. A fun idea is to make a tape recording and play it back. That way you'll know right away which songs sound spectacular and which ones need work. After caroling, hot cocoa and cookies will taste mighty good.

For-the-Birds Party

Remember your neighborhood friends, the birds, by trimming a tree for them. Making the goodies is lots of fun. Watching the feast is, too!

Turn the page to see some treats that birds like and how to make them. After reading the recipes, decide with your mom which steps (such as wiring the pinecones, scooping out the oranges, and popping the corn) to take care of before the party begins. When the treats are "done," put them in a basket or box, bundle up, and take them outside. Pick a tree that you can see from inside your house and attach the goodies securely to the branches.

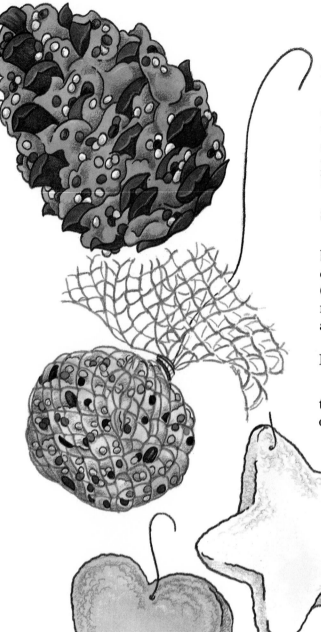

PEANUT-BUTTERED PINECONES

Twist florists' wire around the big ends of pinecones. Mix two parts of peanut butter with one part of suet. Using a spoon, spread the peanut butter mixture on the pinecones. Roll the pinecones in a big bowl of birdseed.

SEED 'N SUET BALLS

Make small balls with a mixture of birdseed, suet, and sunflower seeds. Wrap each ball in a 10″ square of plastic net. (Squares cut from orange bags work nicely.) Gather the corners of the square and wrap with florists' wire.

BREAD SHAPES

Cut shapes from bread with cookie cutters. Attach an ornament hanger or piece of florists' wire to each shape.

GOODY GARLAND

Thread a blunt needle with a piece of nylon fishing line. String bread shapes, cranberries, grapes, apple chunks, and popped corn onto the line.

SWEET TREATS

Attach wire hangers to marshmallows. Loop red ribbon through plain doughnuts and cookies (with holes).

ORANGE BASKETS

Cut oranges in half and scoop out the pulp. On opposite sides of each orange half, poke a hole below the rim. Pull one end of a ribbon through one of the holes and knot it. Pull the other end of the ribbon through the second hole and knot it. Fill the orange with a mixture of birdseed, suet, sunflower seeds, and raisins.

SNACK CUPS

Glue foil baking cups to clip-on clothespins. Fill the cups with birdseed, raisins, and cranberries.

CRANBERRY WREATHS

Cut florists' wire into 18″ pieces. Thread cranberries onto the wire, leaving the ends free. Make a circle with the wire and twist the ends together.

Santa's Workshop Party

Invite your friends for a morning full of fun—making holiday decorations, cards, presents, and trimmings for the tree. When your guests arrive, present each one with a Santa's hat and beard (and your jolliest ho-ho-ho). Ask your mom to make or buy the hats. Cut the beards from batting, as shown on the next page. Be sure to cover the workshop table with a plastic cloth and to have plenty of "tools" on hand. Some suggestions: paper (all kinds and colors), scissors, colored markers, crayons, glue, glitter, stickers, cookie cutters, ribbon, felt, cotton balls, pens and pencils, and *Christmas Is Coming! 1988.* Provide stationery, too, in case someone would like to write Santa. Whistle carols while you work, or play records and sing along.

and Santa's beard. Cut out the pieces. Draw around Santa on red paper, and draw around the hat trim and beard on white paper. Using a hole punch, make two white paper circles for eyes. Cut out a mouth. Glue the pieces onto Santa, and let dry. Using a red pen, write the party information on Santa's beard. Put the invitations in bright green envelopes and send them on their way.

INVITATIONS

Because Christmas is such a busy time, it's a good idea to send invitations early—at least ten days before the party. How long should the party last? About two hours, if you want to serve lunch and play games, too.

To make invitations like the one shown here, trace the outlines of Santa (from head to toe), Santa's hat trim (two pieces),

SANTA BEARDS

For each beard, cut a shape like this from batting. (A good size is 10″ from side to side and 9″ long.) Using small safety pins, pin the ends of the beard to the inside of a Santa hat.

DECORATIONS

With the help of your mom, dad, or an older brother or sister, decorate the "workshop" with streamers, balloons, and paper cutouts. Use patterns in this book or trace shapes from Christmas coloring and activity books.

LUNCH

After working awhile, you and your buddies will be ready for some lunch. A suggested menu (simple, yet scrumptious) appears here.

Cupcake!

Peanut Butter 'n Jam Men Sandwiches

Peanut Butter 'n Jam Men
Fruit Salad
Chips
Hot Cider with
Peppermint Sticks
Santa Cupcakes

To make the sandwiches, use a gingerbread-man cookie cutter to cut shapes from large slices of bread. Spread peanut butter on half the shapes and strawberry jam on the rest. Put the shapes together. Dress the boys in jam vests and the girls in jam dresses. Use raisins for eyes, a mouth, and button trim. Grate a carrot for hair, and glue it on with peanut butter.

To make the cupcakes, frost a batch of cupcakes with white icing. Sprinkle on red sugar for hats and shredded coconut for beards. Use miniature marshmallows for hat pom-poms, chocolate chips for eyes, and red-hot candies for noses.

SANTA SACKS

Serving lunch in Santa sacks will make the meal extra merry. To turn each sack into a Santa, you'll need half of a 5½″ pink circle (for face), a 2½″ white circle and a 1½″ x 6½″ white rectangle (for hat trim), a 1½″ x 5½″ green rectangle and a 2″ yellow square (for belt), two penny-size black circles (for eyes), and a white beard and mustache.

Fold the top corners of the sack to the back. Glue the face about 3¾″ from the top of the sack. Glue on the hat trim and beard. Glue the rest of the pieces in place. Let the glue dry.

Gingerbread Men

GAMES

After lunch, plan to play games. Play your favorites or take your pick from these.

Santa Scramble

Before the party: Print SANTA CLAUS four times on poster paper, writing in large letters and leaving room to cut between the letters. Cut the letters apart, and put them in a bag.

To play: Divide into two teams and sit on the floor. Shake the bag to mix the letters. Pass the bag back and forth between teams, letting each team pick a letter. The first team to spell SANTA CLAUS with its letters, wins.

Santa Says

Play like Simon Says, but Santa's the boss!

Stocking Fill

Before the party: Fill a stocking with 20 small objects (a paper clip, band aid, jingle bell, candy cane, small toy, etc.).

To play: Give each player a pencil and a piece of paper. Empty the stocking, let everyone look at the objects for 30 seconds, and then put everything back in the stocking. Have the players write down the objects. The winner is the one who can remember the most.

Pin the Nose on the Reindeer

Before the party: Make a reindeer like the one on page 39, but leave off the nose. Cover the reindeer with clear self-stick paper, and trim the edges. For each player, make a nose and put a piece of double-stick tape on the back.

To play: Ask a grown-up to tape the reindeer to a door or wall. Blindfold each player in turn, give him a nose, and spin him around. See who can stick the nose closest to where it belongs.

FAVORS

Here's a special favor that friends will love and want to keep forever.

To make the Santa, you'll need a piece of foam core (as big as you are), paint or markers, and a grown-up. Ask the grown-up to draw a Santa on the foam core, leaving the face blank. Color the Santa, and ask the grown-up to cut him out,

with a hole where the face should be.

Before the party, make poster paper frames that are the right size for Polaroid pictures. At the party, take a picture of each guest, standing behind Santa. Pass out the frames. Have everyone tape his picture in place and decorate his frame—to give it a personal touch!

Children's Workshop
Happy Holiday Crafts

Merry Mice

Trace, cut, fold, and glue.
Making these curly-whiskered
fellows is easy to do!

You will need:
Pencil
Tracing paper
Colored paper
Scissors
Hole punch
Ruler
Curling ribbon
Glue stick
Black fine-tip marker

4. Fold the sides of the face up and glue them over the hole. When the glue is dry, fold the ears down. Crease and then unfold the ears.

5. Glue the inner ears and tummy in place. Let the glue dry.

6. For whiskers, cut a 6″ piece of ribbon into three pieces. Glue the pieces to the underside of the mouse's nose, using a paper clip to hold them while the glue dries.

7. Cut a 10″ piece of ribbon for the tail. Glue the tail to the back of the mouse. Let the glue dry.

8. Using the blade of your scissors, gently curl the tail and the ends of the whiskers. Draw eyes with the marker.

1. Trace the patterns, pressing hard with your pencil.

2. Turn the tracings over and retrace them onto sheets of colored paper. Cut out the colored pieces. Cut the circle for the inner ears in half.

3. Fold the top of the mouse down and punch a hole as shown. Cut a 12″ piece of ribbon for a hanger. Pull the ribbon through the holes and tie the ends.

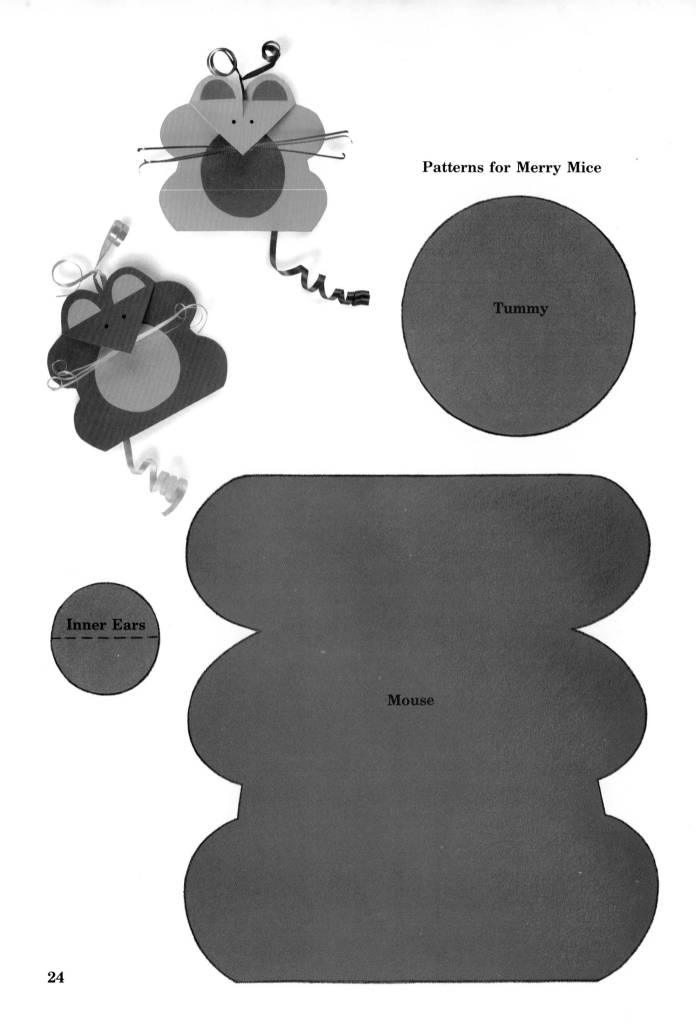

Patterns for Merry Mice

Tummy

Inner Ears

Mouse

Wee Weavings

How merry these will look on your tree! Combine different colors to make each one special.

You will need:
Embroidery floss in different colors
Round toothpicks
Scissors
White glue

1. Using floss that is still attached to the skein, tie two toothpicks together, making an X with the floss. Knot the floss in back of the toothpicks.

2. Follow the drawings to weave the ornament. As you weave, be sure to lay the floss next to, not on top of, the floss that is already in place.

3. When you're ready to change colors, cut the floss. Tie the second color of floss to the end of the first. Begin weaving again, keeping the knot in back.

4. Change colors as often as you like. When the toothpicks are almost covered, wrap the floss around the "top" toothpick several times. Cut the floss and glue the end to the back of the toothpick. Let dry.

5. Cut a piece of floss for a hanger. Glue the ends to the back of the top toothpick. Let the glue dry.

Level 2

25

Sparkly Snowmen

What makes these so lovable? Pom-pom noses, a pudgy shape, and great big toothy smiles!

You will need:
Pencil
Tracing paper
Scissors
2 (5″ x 5½″) pieces of white felt
Straight pins
Scraps of colored felt, fabric, and ribbon
Pinking shears
3 cotton balls
White glue
Small plastic buttons (or a hole punch to make felt buttons)
Small white pom-pom
Black slick pen
Clear glitter
Fishing line

1. Trace and cut out the patterns.

2. Stack the white felt pieces and pin the snowman to them. Pin the hat to a scrap of colored felt. Cut out the felt pieces. Using the pinking shears, cut the scarf from a fabric scrap.

3. Put the cotton balls on one snowman's tummy. Run a line of glue around the snowman's edges and place the other snowman on top. Pinch the edges of the snowmen together. Let the glue dry.

4. Glue the hat to the snowman's head. Cut a piece of ribbon for a hatband. Cut a tiny holly leaf and some berries from green and red felt. Glue the pieces to the hat and let dry.

5. Glue the scarf, buttons, and pom-pom nose in place. Let the glue dry.

6. Practice drawing dots on a scrap of felt, using the slick pen. Then draw two eyes and a mouth on the snowman. Let the paint dry.

7. Spread glue on the snowman and sprinkle him with glitter. When the glue is dry, shake off the excess glitter.

8. Use a pin to punch a hole in the top of the snowman's hat. Pull a piece of fishing line through the hole and tie the ends for a hanger.

Hat

Snowman

Scarf

Yarn-Wrapped Wreath

Use bright green yarn to fashion this wreath. Add shiny red buttons for berries.

You will need:
Pencil
Coffee can lid
6″ square of white poster paper
Scissors
Small jar (about 2″ across)
Tape measure
Thick green yarn
24″ piece of ribbon
Tacky glue
Red buttons
Fishing line

1. Draw around the lid on poster paper. Place the jar in the middle of the circle. Draw around the jar. Cut out the circles to make a wreath.

2. Cut twelve pieces of yarn about 18″ long. Wrap one piece of yarn around the wreath, leaving 1″ of yarn on the back of the wreath. Wrap another piece of yarn around the wreath, catching the 1″ end of the first piece. Keep wrapping the wreath with yarn until the wreath is covered, tucking any loose ends under the wrapped yarn.

3. Tie the ribbon into a bow and glue it to the top of the wreath. Glue on the buttons for berries. Let the glue dry.

4. Cut a piece of fishing line for a hanger. Run the fishing line under some yarn at the top of the wreath and tie the ends.

Polka-Dot Bird

How Christmasy this perky bird looks—as if he's all dressed up for a party!

You will need:
Glue stick
2 (4″ x 6½″) pieces of polka-dot wrapping paper
4″ x 6½″ piece of poster paper
Pencil
Tracing paper
Scissors
Hole punch
5½″ x 14″ piece of tissue paper
2 reinforcement tabs (round with holes)
String

1. Glue the wrapping paper to both sides of the poster paper. Let the glue dry.

2. Trace the pattern for the bird. Cut out the pattern and draw around it on the poster paper. Cut out the bird.

3. Ask a grownup to cut the slit in the bird for the wings. Punch a hole above the slit with the hole punch.

4. To make the wings, fold the tissue paper as though you were making a fan. Pull the wings through the slit.

5. Punch a hole for the bird's eye. Stick a reinforcement tab over the hole on each side of the bird.

6. Pull the string through the hole above the wings. Tie the ends for a hanger.

Bird

Cut slit here.

Level 1

29

Dip-and-Drape Angel

An ornament this sweet will be the star of any tree. Follow the steps and watch with surprise as your angel takes shape.

Before you start: The more you handle the dampened Dip-'N-Drape pieces, the less sticky they become, so dress your angel quickly. If you cannot find Dip-'N-Drape fabric, use regular fabric and liquid fabric stiffener.

You will need:
Pencil
Tracing paper
Scissors
8½" x 10½" white poster paper
10½" x 17" Dip-'N-Drape fabric
Waxed paper
Bowl of water
Toothpick
Paintbrushes
Gesso
Acrylic paint (white, blue, flesh, and yellow)
Fine-tip markers (blue, brown, and red)
Clear plastic spray enamel
Narrow ribbon
White glue
Gold embroidery floss (for hanger)

1. Trace and cut out the patterns. Cut out the pieces as marked.

2. Tear off small and medium-size pieces of waxed paper for stuffing the dress sleeves and skirt. Crumple the pieces.

3. Gently crumple the waxed paper face (for padding) and lay it on the poster paper angel's face. Dip the Dip-'N-Drape face quickly in water and then wrap it around the poster paper face, covering the waxed paper.

4. Line the angel's arms and body with the crumpled waxed paper. Dampen one dress piece and drape it over the angel, gathering the dress piece at the neck. Gently turn the angel over.

    Line the back of the angel with crumpled waxed paper. Dampen and drape the second dress piece, overlapping the edges with the front dress piece.

5. Dampen the hair and drape it over the angel's head. Use the toothpick to separate and arrange the strands. (If a strand breaks off, just stick it back on.)

6. Dip the Dip-'N-Drape halo and stick it on the poster paper halo. Press the halo (Dip-'N-Drape side) onto the back of the angel's head.

7. Dip the Dip-'N-Drape wings and stick them onto the poster paper wings. Press the wings (Dip-'N-Drape side) onto the back of the angel. Let the angel dry overnight.

8. Paint the entire angel with gesso and let dry. Paint the angel with several coats of paint, using one color at a time and letting the paint dry between coats. When the angel is dry, draw the face with the markers. Spray the angel with the clear plastic enamel and let dry.

9. Tie the ribbon into a bow and glue it to the neck of the dress. Glue the ends of the floss to the back of the halo. Let the glue dry.

Angel

Cut 1 from poster paper.

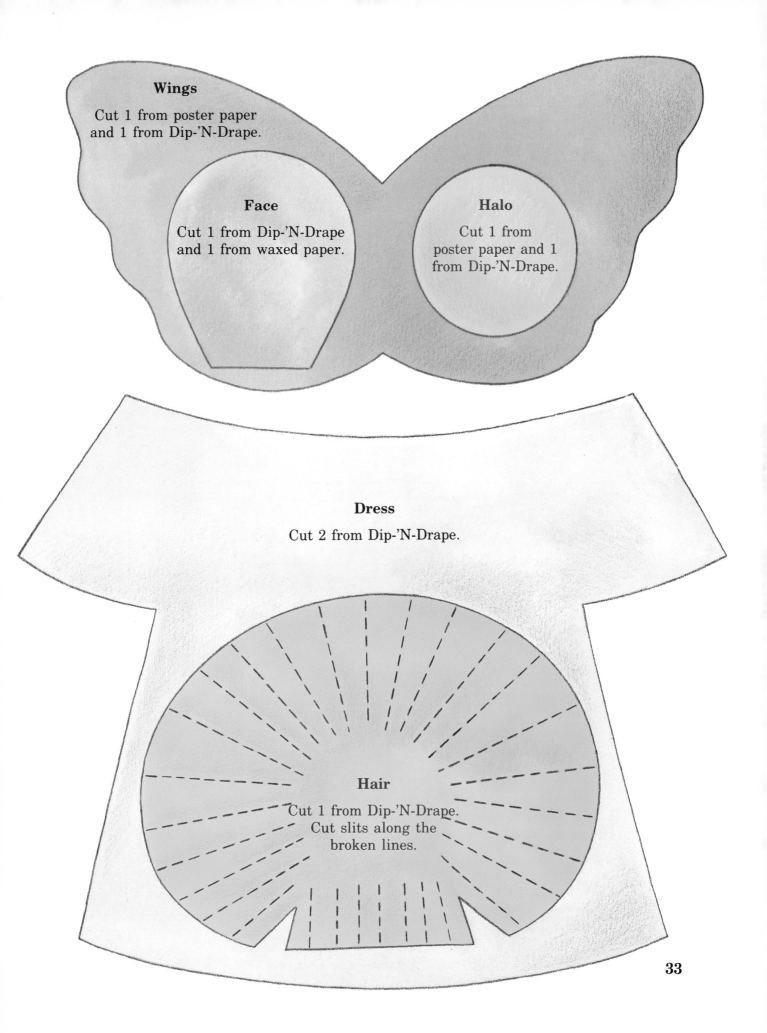

Wings

Cut 1 from poster paper
and 1 from Dip-'N-Drape.

Face

Cut 1 from Dip-'N-Drape
and 1 from waxed paper.

Halo

Cut 1 from
poster paper and 1
from Dip-'N-Drape.

Dress

Cut 2 from Dip-'N-Drape.

Hair

Cut 1 from Dip-'N-Drape.
Cut slits along the
broken lines.

Soapbox Soldier

Stand this smart soldier under your tree. He'll guard the gifts till Christmas day!

You will need:
Pencil
Ruler
1 (42-ounce) round oatmeal box
Tempera paint (red, white, and black)
Paintbrush
Tracing paper
Scissors
Black poster paper
Wrapping paper (red, blue, and scrap of green)
Black construction paper
A nickel and a quarter
2 brads
⅝"-wide gold ribbon (about 1½ yards)
Tape measure
White glue
2 (72-ounce) detergent boxes
Masking, clear, and double-stick tape
2½" piece of 1¼"-wide gold ribbon
Paper clips
¼"-wide gold ribbon (about 1 yard)
2 paper towel rolls
12" piece of gold garland

Making the Head

1. For the face, draw a 4½" x 5½" rectangle, starting at the bottom edge of the oatmeal box. Mix the red and white paint to make pink. Paint the face and let dry. Paint the rest of the box and the top black. Let the paint dry.

2. Trace and cut out the patterns for the hat brim, mouth, and mustache. Cut the pieces as marked. On construction paper, draw around the nickel twice for eyes. Cut out the pieces.

3. Fold the ends of the hat brim up. While you hold the brim in place, ask a grown-up to poke a hole through each end, going through the box. Attach the brim to the box with the brads.

4. Glue the eyes, mouth, and mustache in place. Let the glue dry.

5. From the ⅝"-wide gold ribbon, cut an 18" piece for the hatband and a 14½" piece for the chin strap. Glue the hatband around the box above the brim. Glue the ends of the chin strap to the box below the brim. Let the glue dry.

Making the Body

1. Trace and cut out the patterns for the gloves, shoes, and leg divider. Cut the pieces as marked. From the poster paper, cut one

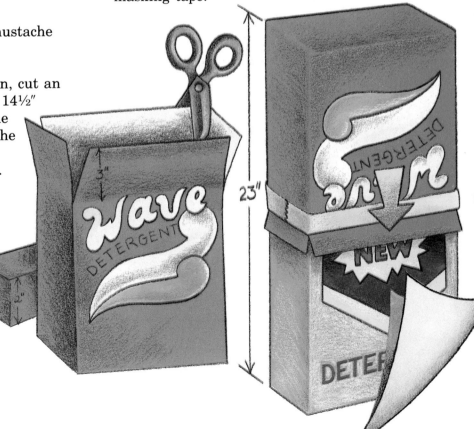

1¼" x 25" strip for the belt and one 1¼" x 2" rectangle for the belt buckle.

2. Measure 2" down from the top of one detergent box. Cut off this section of the box. Then cut a 3" slit down each top corner. Turn the box upside down and slip it over the other detergent box. (Together the boxes should measure about 23" high, with the top box being 10" and the bottom box 13".) Tape the boxes together with masking tape.

3. Measure 10″ down from the top of the box and draw a line around the box. Wrap the box below the line with blue wrapping paper. Wrap the box above the line with red wrapping paper.

4. Wrap the belt around the soldier's waist and tape the ends in back with clear tape. Glue the piece of 1¼″-wide gold ribbon to the poster paper buckle. Glue the buckle to the front of the belt, using paper clips to hold the buckle while the glue dries.

5. Glue the straight edges of the shoes to the bottom of the box. Cut four 2″ pieces of ¼″-wide gold ribbon. Glue two ribbon pieces to the top of each shoe. Glue the leg divider in place. Let the glue dry.

6. Cut two 9″ pieces of ⅝″-wide gold ribbon. Glue the ribbons to the soldier's chest, crisscrossing them. Draw around the quarter four times on the green paper. Cut out the circles and glue them to the ends of the ribbons.

7. Wrap the paper towel rolls with red wrapping paper. At one end of each roll, glue two rows of narrow gold ribbon. Tape the rolls to the box for arms, running the tape inside the rolls.

8. Spread glue along the straight edge of each glove. Gently fold the gloves and stick them inside the sleeves. Let the glue dry.

9. Run a piece of double-stick tape across the top of the body and another piece across the bottom of the head, centering the tape. Stick the head on the body and press. Cut the garland in half and stick a piece along each shoulder, to cover the holes in the paper towel rolls.

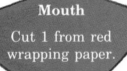

Mouth

Cut 1 from red
wrapping paper.

Hat Brim

Cut 1 from black poster paper.

Mustache

Cut 1
from black
construction
paper.

Gloves and Shoes

Cut 2 gloves from black construction
paper.
Cut 2 shoes from black poster paper.

Leg Divider

Cut 1 from black
construction paper.

Paper Reindeer

Who "nose" this reindeer's name?

You will need:
Pencil
Tracing paper
Scissors
Construction paper in assorted colors
  (including red, white, brown, and tan)
Salad plate
Hole punch
White glue
Black felt-tip marker

1. Trace and cut out the patterns.

2. Draw around the nose on red paper and the hat trim and hat tuft on white paper. Draw around the antler two times on brown paper. Draw around the hat on any color of paper you like. For the head, draw around the salad plate on tan paper. Cut out the paper pieces.

3. Punch circles from white paper. Glue the trim, tuft, and circles to the hat.

4. Glue the hat and nose to the front of the head. Glue the antlers to the back of the head. Let the glue dry.

5. Use the marker to draw two eyes and a big smile.

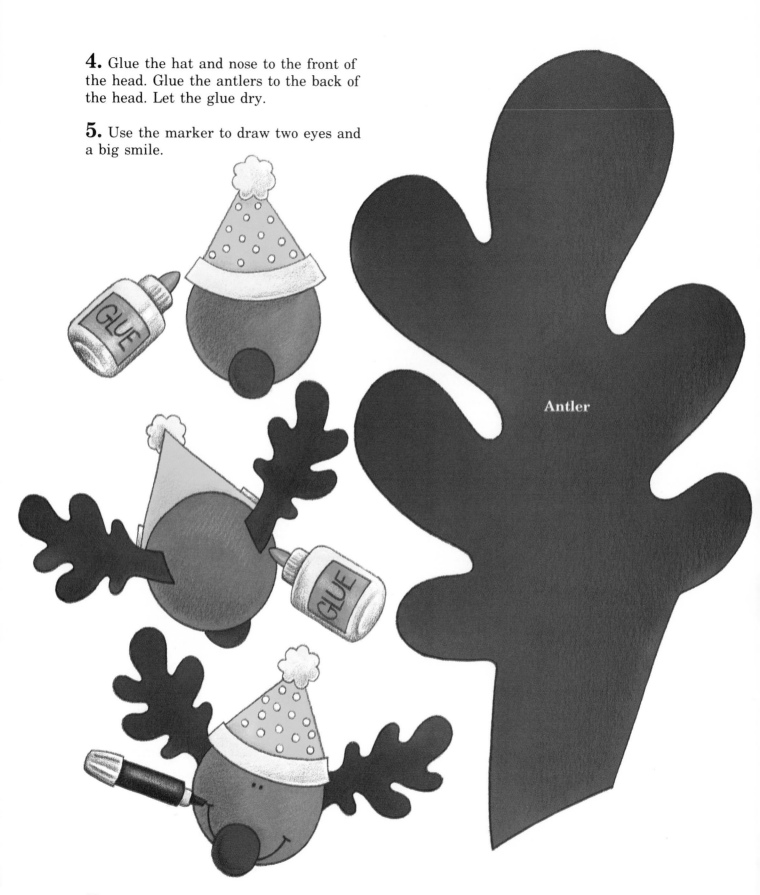

Antler

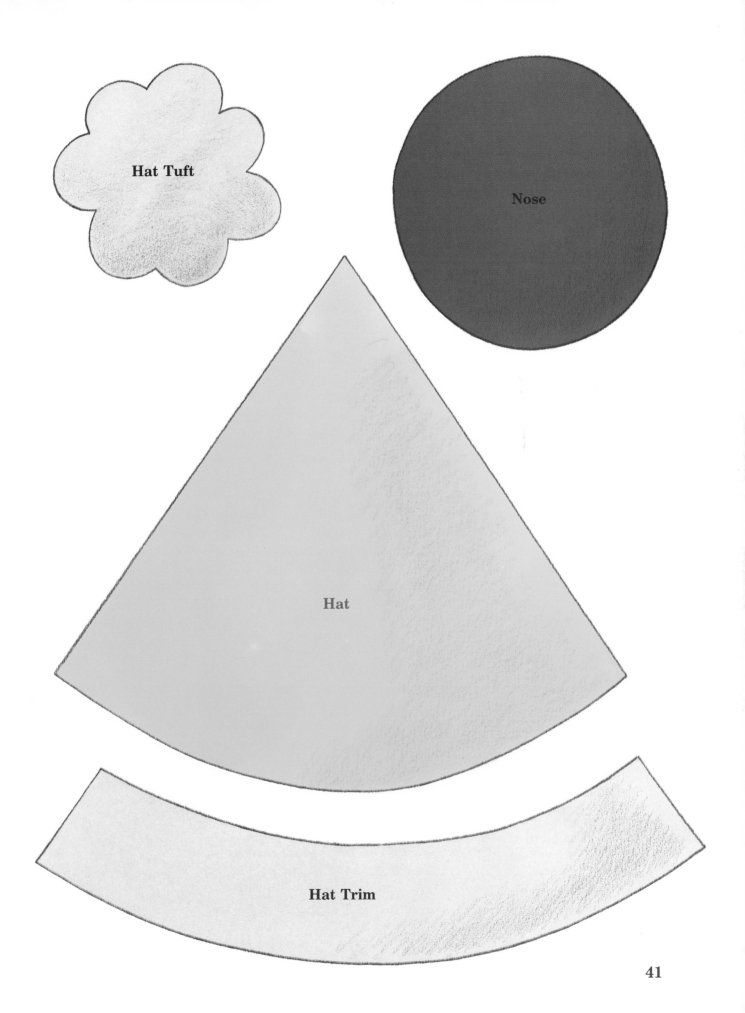

Hat Tuft

Nose

Hat

Hat Trim

Away in a Manger

Celebrate Jesus' birthday with a special family project. Mom can sew the puppets, and Dad can help you build the stable. On Christmas Eve, have a play for family and friends.

You will need:
Pencil
Tracing paper
Scissors
Scraps of fabric, felt, lightweight fusible interfacing, and poster paper
Thread to match fabrics
Sewing machine and an iron
Black and brown fine-tip markers (permanent)
Cotton swab and powdered blush
Tacky Glue
Waxed paper
Stuffing
20 jumbo (¾″ x 5½″) craft sticks
Glitter
Ruler and yardstick
Paintbrushes
Wood stain
Packing straw
Heavy cardboard box (at least 21″ x 9″ x 16″ high)
8½″ x 11″ piece of typing paper
Clear tape
Self-stick paper (textured look)
  Textured and acrylic paint

For safety's sake: Use the sewing machine and iron only with a grown-up's permission.

Making the Puppets and Star

1. Trace and cut out the patterns. Cut the pieces as marked.

2. To make Mary, Joseph, and the Angel, sew the two pieces for each body with right sides together, leaving the bottom edges open. Turn the bodies right side out and press them with the iron. Hem the bottom edges.

Place the interfacing faces, rough side down, over the patterns in the book and trace the features, using the black marker. Color the eyes brown. Rub blush on the cheeks with the cotton swab.

Set the iron on permanent press. Place the interfacing faces, rough side down, on the felt faces and fuse them. Glue the hair in place. Put waxed paper inside the puppets. Glue the faces and the angel's wings in place. When the glue is dry, remove the paper.

3. Sew the two pieces for Baby Jesus' body, leaving an opening as marked. Turn the body right side out and press. Lightly stuff the body, keeping it flat. Turn the edges of the opening under and sew them closed.

Make Baby Jesus' face as in step 2. Glue the head covering to the face and glue the face to the body. Let dry.

4. To make the animals, place the interfacing bodies over the patterns in the book and trace the lines with the black marker. Color the cow's eye and nose brown. Rub blush on the cow's cheek. Fuse the interfacing bodies to the felt bodies.

Glue the sheep's faces to the poster paper bodies. Glue the felt bodies to the poster paper bodies and glue the legs on the back. Cut spots from felt for the cow. Glue the spots and remaining felt pieces in place. Glue two craft sticks to the back of each animal, lining up the sticks with the legs. Let the glue dry.

5. Glue the felt star to the poster paper star. Run glue along the outer edges of the star and sprinkle them with glitter. Let the glue dry.

Making the Manger

1. To make the manger legs, draw a line across four craft sticks, 1¾″ from one end. Glue the sticks in pairs, crossing them at the lines. Let the glue dry.

2. Ask someone to stand the legs 3″ apart, with the little Vs down and the big Vs up. Run a line of glue along the inside edges of the big Vs. Glue four craft sticks, side by side, to each side of the V. Let the glue dry.

3. Stain the manger and let dry. Fill the manger with straw.

2. To make a pattern for the doorway, fold the typing paper in half and cut a curve as shown. Open the pattern and center it along the bottom of the stable front. Draw around the pattern.

3. On the stable front, find the center of the top edge and mark it with an X. Measure and mark 10″ up from the bottom of each front corner. Draw a line from each 10″ mark to the X. Then draw a line across the sides of the stable, 10″ from the bottom edge.

Making the Stable

1. If the box has a top, cut if off. Turn the box so that the bottom of it becomes the stable front.

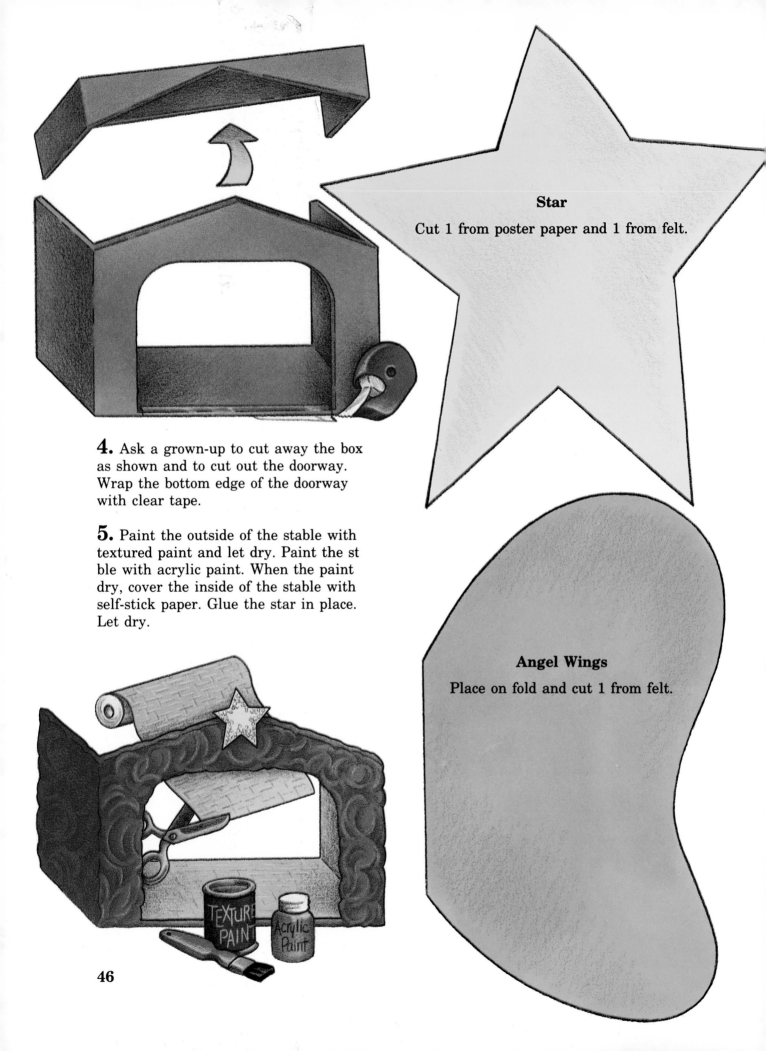

4. Ask a grown-up to cut away the box as shown and to cut out the doorway. Wrap the bottom edge of the doorway with clear tape.

5. Paint the outside of the stable with textured paint and let dry. Paint the st ble with acrylic paint. When the paint dry, cover the inside of the stable with self-stick paper. Glue the star in place. Let dry.

Star

Cut 1 from poster paper and 1 from felt.

Angel Wings

Place on fold and cut 1 from felt.

Joseph Face

Cut 1 from felt and
1 from interfacing.

Joseph Hair and Beard

Cut 1 from felt.

Mary and Angel Face

For each puppet, cut 1 from felt and 1
from interfacing.

Baby Jesus Face

Cut 1 from felt and 1 from interfacing.

Leave open.

Baby Jesus Body

Add ¼″ seam allowance
all around.
Cut 2 from fabric.

**Baby Jesus
Head Covering**

Mary, Joseph, and Angel Body

Add ¼″ seam allowance all around.
For each puppet, cut 2 from fabric.

Leave open.

Cut 1 from felt.

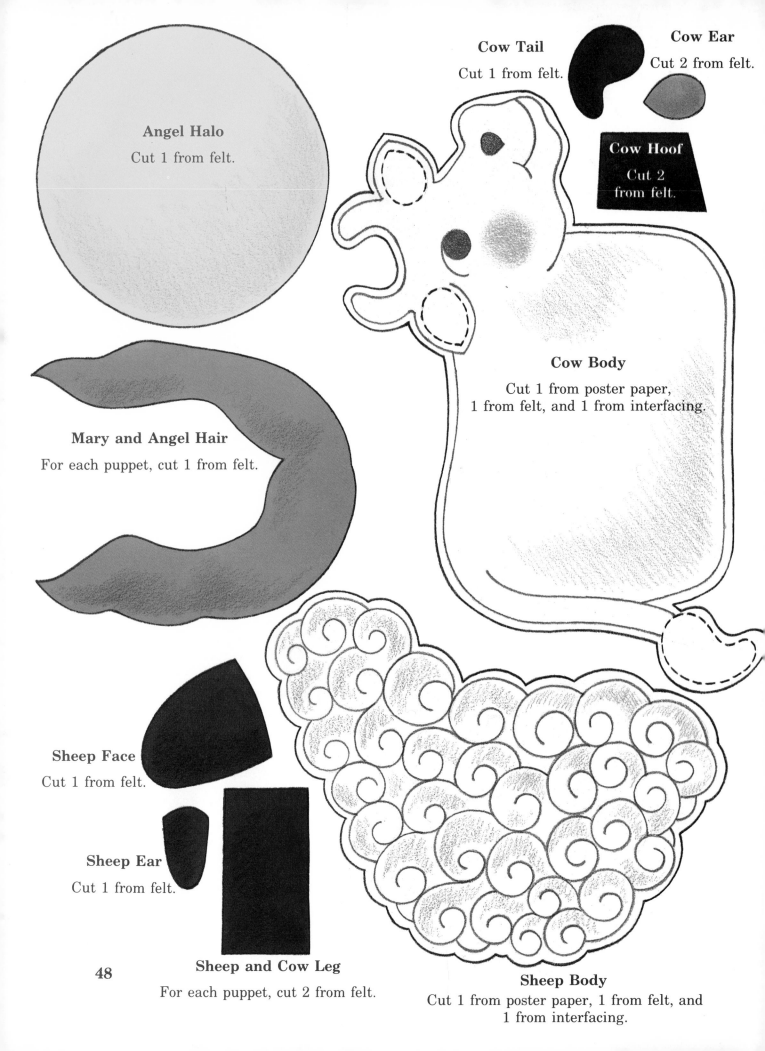

Angel Halo

Cut 1 from felt.

Cow Tail

Cut 1 from felt.

Cow Ear

Cut 2 from felt.

Cow Hoof

Cut 2 from felt.

Cow Body

Cut 1 from poster paper,
1 from felt, and 1 from interfacing.

Mary and Angel Hair

For each puppet, cut 1 from felt.

Sheep Face

Cut 1 from felt.

Sheep Ear

Cut 1 from felt.

48

Sheep and Cow Leg

For each puppet, cut 2 from felt.

Sheep Body

Cut 1 from poster paper, 1 from felt, and
1 from interfacing.

Angel Wrap

Here's a pretty wrapping for a present. Angel boxes make heavenly decorations, too!

You will need:
Pencil
Tracing paper
White poster paper
Scissors
5″ x 7″ piece of wrapping paper for sleeves
Pink construction paper
Glue stick
Tape measure
Curling ribbon
Black and red fine-tip markers
Clear tape
Wrapped box (not over 6½″ wide)
12″ x 27″ piece of wrapping paper for wings
⅔ yard of cording
White glue
Glitter

Level 2

1. Trace the patterns, pressing hard with your pencil. Turn the tracings over and retrace them onto the poster paper. Cut out the pieces. Ask a grown-up to cut a slit in the halo.

2. Draw around the sleeves on the small piece of wrapping paper. Draw around the head and hands on the pink paper. Cut out the pieces and glue them to the poster paper pieces. Let the glue dry.

3. Cut 16 two-inch pieces of ribbon for hair. Curl one end of each ribbon piece, using the blade of your scissors. Glue the hair to the angel's head as shown. When the glue is dry, trim the straight ends of the hair, following the shape of the head. Use the markers to draw a face.

4. Gently fold the head tab toward the back of the head. Tape the tab to the box so that the head stands up.

5. Fold the large piece of wrapping paper in half with the short edges together. Pleat the paper to make the wings. Center the wings behind the angel's head and tape them in place. On either side of the box, pull the last pleat down and tape it.

6. Gently fold the hands and tape the tabs to the backs of the sleeves. Glue cording along the curved edges of the sleeves, using white glue. When the glue is dry, tape the sleeves to the box.

7. Spread one side of the halo with glue and sprinkle it with glitter. Run a thin line of white glue along the outer edges of the wings and sprinkle them with glitter. When the glue is dry, shake off the glitter that did not stick. Slip the halo on the angel's head.

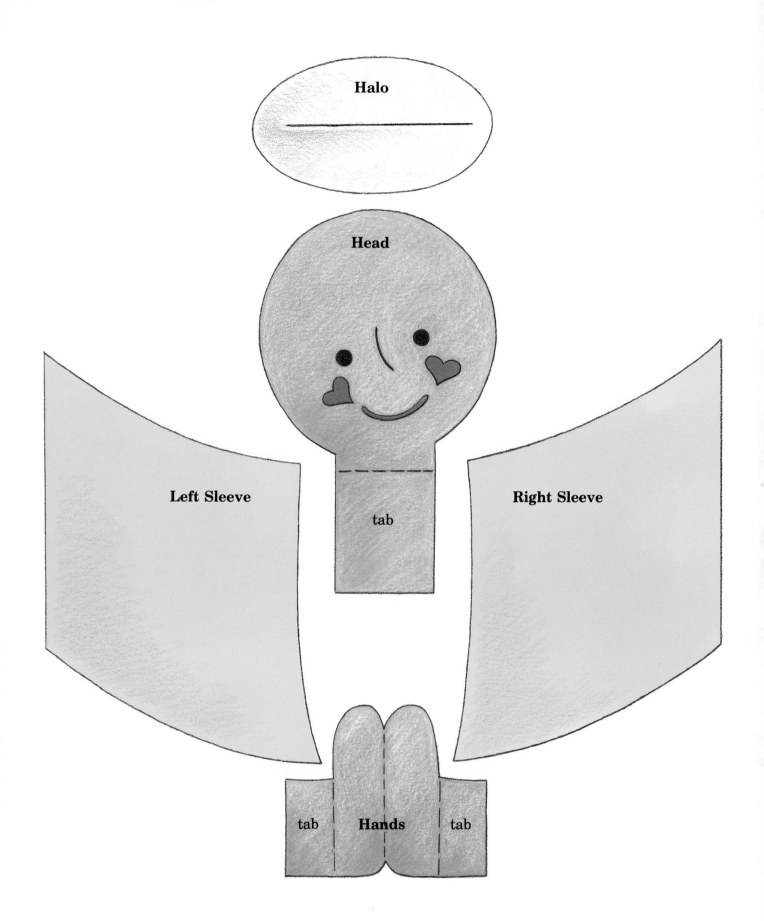

51

One-of-a-Kind Cards

Create cards for your friends at school—quick as a wink, with printers' ink!

You will need:

6½″ x 9½″ piece of white construction paper
Newspaper
Cookie sheet
Water-soluble printers' ink
Printers' brayer
4½″ x 6″ piece of poster paper (1 for each color of ink)
Pencil with eraser
Paper towels

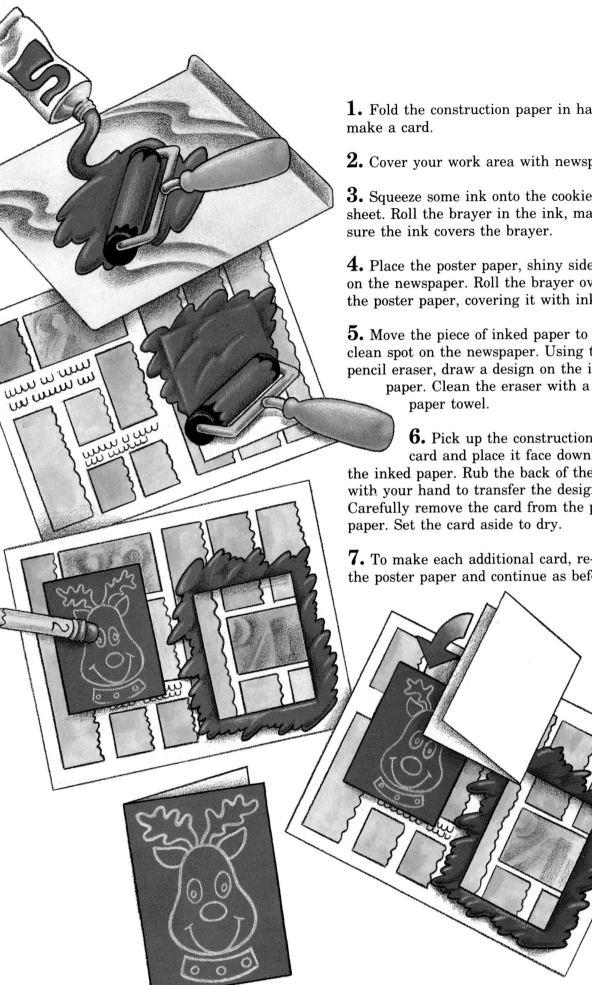

1. Fold the construction paper in half to make a card.

2. Cover your work area with newspaper.

3. Squeeze some ink onto the cookie sheet. Roll the brayer in the ink, making sure the ink covers the brayer.

4. Place the poster paper, shiny side up, on the newspaper. Roll the brayer over the poster paper, covering it with ink.

5. Move the piece of inked paper to a clean spot on the newspaper. Using the pencil eraser, draw a design on the inked paper. Clean the eraser with a paper towel.

6. Pick up the construction paper card and place it face down on the inked paper. Rub the back of the card with your hand to transfer the design. Carefully remove the card from the poster paper. Set the card aside to dry.

7. To make each additional card, re-ink the poster paper and continue as before.

Photo Fun

For folks who haven't seen you in a while, these cards and gift tags are picture-perfect!

Level 1

You will need:
Pencil
Assortment of poster paper, construction
    paper, and wrapping paper
Scissors
Glue stick
Photographs
Colored markers
Ribbon

1. To make a gift tag, draw a shape on poster paper. Cut out the shape and decorate it with your photograph, paper cutouts, and markers. Use ribbon for a tie.

2. To make a card, cut and fold a piece of poster paper. Decorate the card with photographs, paper cutouts, and markers.

55

Stocking Wrap

Turn an ordinary sack into a super wrap with ribbon, paper cutouts, glitter, and glue!

You will need:
Pencil
Tracing paper
Scissors
Large grocery sack
5″ x 6″ piece of green construction paper
Glue stick
Sequins, glitter, little bows, and other decorations
Construction paper in green, yellow, and other colors
Hole punch
Curling ribbon

1. Trace and cut out the stocking and star patterns on the facing page.

2. Cut the bottom off the sack and smooth the sack out flat.

3. Place the stocking pattern on the folded edge of the sack as shown and draw around it, drawing the stocking as tall as you like. Cut out the stocking. (Do not cut along the fold.)

4. Fold the piece of green paper in half and cut out half a tree. Open the tree and glue it to the stocking. Decorate the tree.

5. Draw around the star pattern on yellow paper. Cut out the star and glue it to the top of the tree.

6. Cut out some paper presents and glue them to the stocking. Glue bows to the presents.

7. Glue the curved edges of the stocking together, leaving the top open. Let dry.

8. Punch two holes several inches apart in the top of the stocking. Put your gift inside the stocking. Cut several pieces of curling ribbon and pull them through the holes. Tie the ribbons and curl the ends.

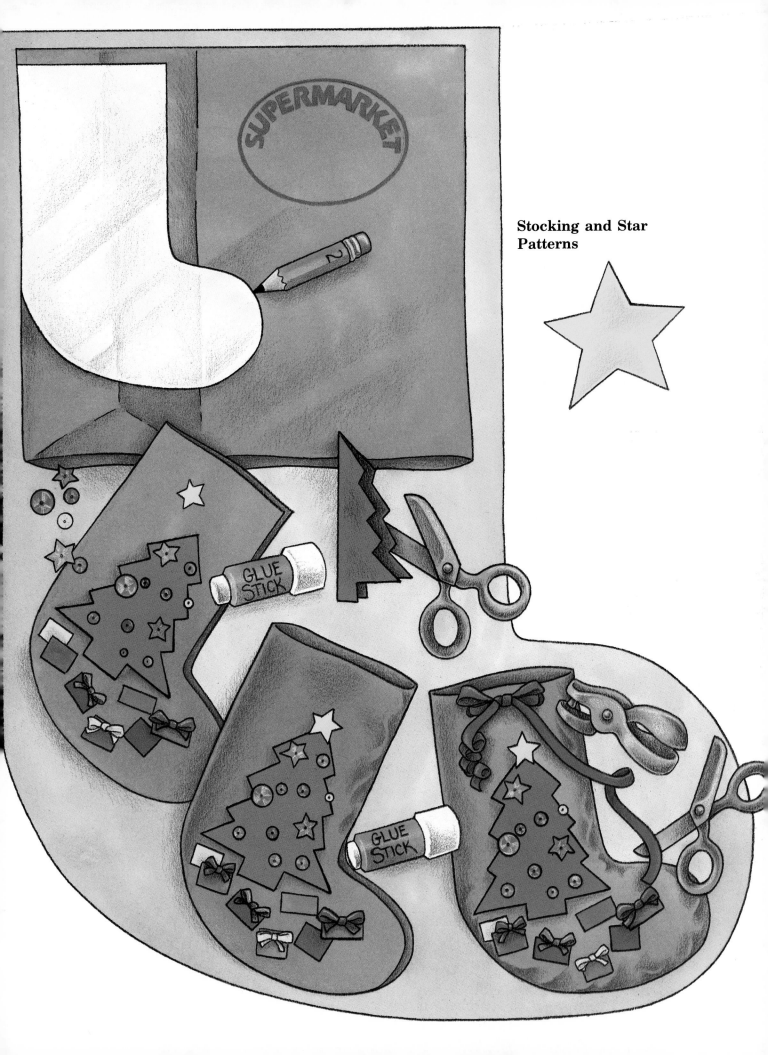

Stocking and Star Patterns

Car Wash Kit

Looking for a nifty gift for your dad? It's a bet this will be a big hit!

You will need:
Pencil
Tracing paper
Scissors
Grease pencil (or china marker)
Bucket
Small dustpan and whisk broom
Plastic squeeze bottle
Sandpaper (fine)
Chamois cloth
Scrub brush
Squeegee
Masking tape
Tape measure
Acrylic paint
Paintbrush
Liquid detergent (mild)
Paper and markers for making coupon
Sponge

1. Trace the letters for "Dad" and cut them out.

2. Using the grease pencil, draw around the letters on the bucket, dustpan, and squeeze bottle. Rough up the letters (inside the outline), using sandpaper.

3. Draw around the letters on the chamois cloth and the scrub brush with the pencil.

4. Use strips of masking tape to mark the areas that you would like to stripe. Measure to be sure that the tape is on straight.

5. Paint the squeegee and scrub brush handles. Let the paint dry.

6. Paint the letters and the stripes. When the paint is dry, remove the tape.

7. Fill the squeeze bottle with liquid detergent. Make a "Free Car Wash" coupon. Put the cleaning items and the coupon in the bucket.

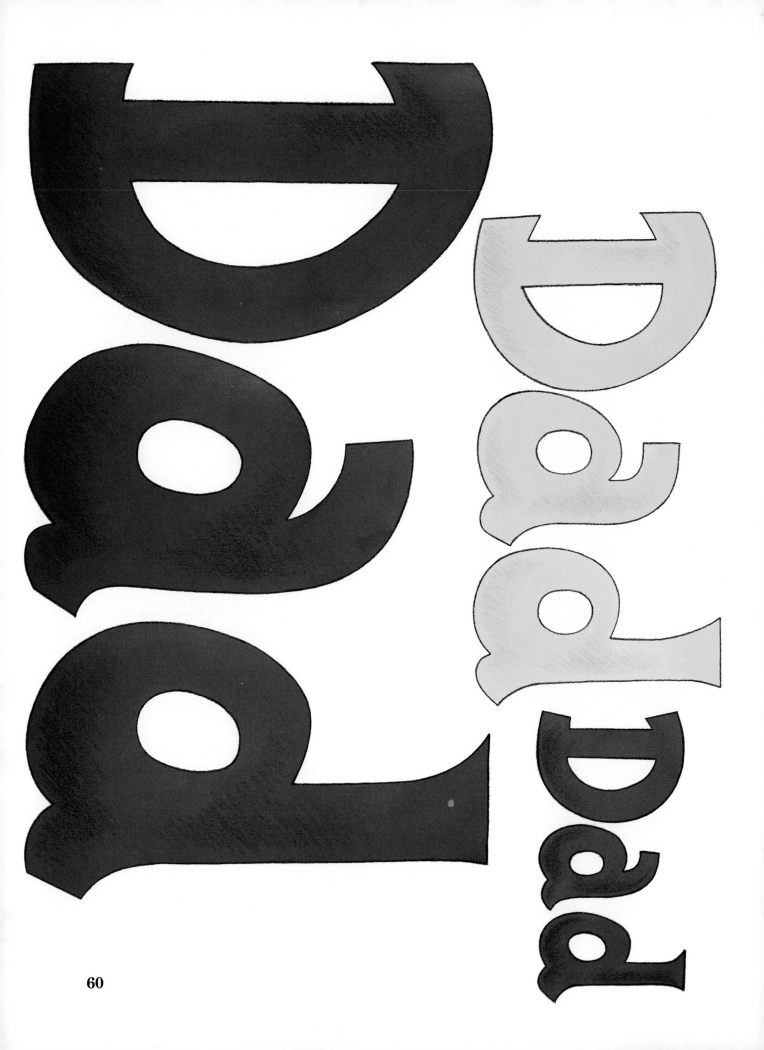

60

Tip-Toppers

Treat your teacher to a goodie-filled jar, topped off with a decorated dough-covered lid!

For safety's sake: Ask a grown-up to help make the dough and bake the lids.

You will need:
2¼ cups water
2 cups salt
3 cups white flour
1 cup whole wheat flour
Saucepan
Wooden spoon
Mixing bowl
6 to 9 jars with metal lids
Butter knife, spoon, fork, and toothpick
Tiny aspic cutters
Cookie sheet
Colored markers
Clear plastic spray enamel
Candy sprinkles
White glue
Peppermints and tiny bows
Small ornaments
⅝"-wide ribbon in different colors

Level 3

1. Bring the water to a boil in the sauce-pan. Take the pan off the heat and add the salt.

2. Mix the white and wheat flours in the mixing bowl. Add the water and salt mixture and stir.

3. Sprinkle your work surface lightly with flour. Knead the dough until smooth.

4. Separate the dough into six to nine balls, saving some dough for cutouts. Shape a dough ball over each lid, keeping the dough as thin as possible. (The thinner the dough, the shorter the drying time.)

5. Using the knife, spoon, fork, and toothpick, make decorative holes and cuts on the dough-covered lids. Cut shapes from the remaining dough, using the aspic cutters. Stick the shapes on the lids.

6. Place the lids on a cookie sheet. Bake the lids in a 250° oven for two to three hours or until dry. (Check the lids every 20 minutes after two hours.) Remove the cookie sheet from the oven. Let the lids cool.

7. Use the markers to decorate the lids and to color the cutouts.

8. To add the sprinkles, spray the topper with the clear plastic enamel. While the topper is still wet, sprinkle it with sprinkles. Let dry and spray again.

   To add the peppermints and bows, glue the candies to the topper and let dry. Spray the topper with the clear plastic enamel and let dry. Glue the bows to the candies. Let the glue dry.

   To add ornaments, simply glue them in place. Let the glue dry.

9. Fill the jars with goodies. Gently screw on the lids. Tie a ribbon around each jar.

Froggie Bank

Friends will flip for this funny frog, who'd rather have a dime than a juicy beetle bug!

You will need:
Ruler
4½″ square box (or bigger)
Pencil
Tracing paper
Poster paper (about 12″ x 18″)
Scissors
Glue stick
Green wrapping paper
Clear tape
24″ (1″-wide) ribbon
Hole punch
Scrap of blue paper
6″ yellow chenille stem
2 table tennis balls
2 large wiggly-eyes

Before you start: Measure the top front edge of your box. If the edge is longer than 4½″, you'll need to draw a face for your frog, rather than using the pattern that is given. Make the straight edge on the face the same length as the edge of your box.

1. Trace the foot and face patterns, pressing hard with your pencil. Turn the tracings over and retrace them onto the poster paper. Cut out the poster paper pieces.

2. Glue the poster paper pieces to a piece of the green wrapping paper. When the glue is dry, cut around the shapes.

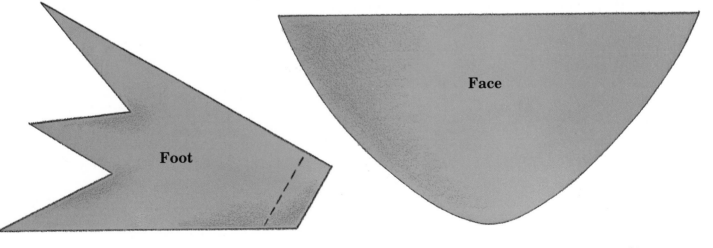

3. Wrap the box with green wrapping paper. Tape the face to the box as shown. Glue the feet to the bottom of the box. When the glue is dry, tape the feet to make sure they stay in place.

4. Measure one side of the box. For legs, cut two poster paper rectangles that are as wide as your box and 12″ long.

5. Draw around each leg two times on the wrapping paper. Cut out the wrapping paper legs and glue them to both sides of the poster paper legs. Let the glue dry.

6. Glue one end of each leg to the box as shown. Tie the ribbon around the box and

legs, and make a bow. Let the glue dry. Bring the other ends of the legs to the bottom edge of the box and tape them in place.

7. Punch holes in the blue paper. Glue the circles to the face and legs. Curl one end of the chenille stem and glue the other end to the underside of the face. Glue the table tennis balls to the top of the box. Let the glue dry.

8. Lay the frog on its back. Glue the wiggly-eyes to the table tennis balls and let dry.

9. Ask a grown-up to make an opening for money in the top of the box.

Foot

Face

Buttons 'n Beads Jewelry

Cute as can be, these jewelry sets take just minutes to make. Here's how!

For safety's sake: Use Krazy Glue only with a grown-up's permission. Be sure to read the directions on the Krazy Glue container and follow them carefully.

You will need:
¾ yard (⅛"-wide) satin ribbon
Tape measure
Tapestry needle
Small novelty buttons (shank-type) and
   wooden beads
28" piece of elastic thread
Krazy Glue
Adjustable ring with round disk
Pierced-earring posts (hypo-allergenic)
Bobby pins

1. To make a necklace, tie a double knot in the ribbon, 6″ from one end. Thread the needle with the other ribbon end. String beads and buttons onto the ribbon, leaving 6″ of ribbon free. At the last bead, tie a double knot in the ribbon. Tie a button onto each ribbon end, if you like.

2. To make a bracelet, thread the needle with the elastic thread. Pull the ends of the thread so they're even and tie them together in a triple knot. String 6″ to 7″ of the doubled thread with beads and buttons. When you're through, run the needle through all the beads and buttons again, starting with the first bead you strung. Securely tie the thread to the knotted end as shown. Cut the thread to release the needle.

3. To make a ring, earrings, and decorated bobby pins, ask a grown-up to cut the shanks off the buttons that you would like to use. Glue the buttons to the ring disk, earring posts, and bobby pins. Let the glue dry overnight.

Stickum-Ups

Rub-a-dub-dub! Little brothers and sisters will love playing in the tub with these shiny shapes.

You will need:
Pencil
Cookie cutters
Wrapping paper
Scissors
Clear self-stick paper

1. Draw around the cookie cutters on the wrapping paper. Cut out the shapes.

2. Lay a piece of self-stick paper, sticky side up, on the table.

3. Place the shapes 1″ apart on the self-stick paper and smooth another piece of self-stick paper, sticky side down, on top.

4. Cut out the shapes, leaving a border of self-stick paper around each wrapping paper shape.

Parents' Workshop
Great Gifts for Children

Snowy Day Appliqué

Right at home on a Christmas-red dress, this pieced appliqué will see a girl through the holiday season.

You will need:
Garment to be appliquéd
½ yard lightweight fusible interfacing
Fabric scraps
Thread to match
6″ (⅛″-wide) ribbon
1 small heart button

1. Fuse pieces of interfacing to wrong side of fabric scraps. Transfer patterns to scraps and cut out pieces.

2. Determine placement of appliqué on garment and cut one piece of interfacing large enough to back entire appliqué. On wrong side of garment, position and fuse piece of interfacing.

3. Set sewing machine for appliqué. Using satin stitch, appliqué pieces in the following order: house (bottom and two side edges only), left rooftop, right rooftop, middle rooftop, door, windows, wreath, trees, snowman, scarf, and hat.

4. Topstitch house and windows as marked on patterns. Tie ribbon into bow and tack to wreath; trim ends. Sew button to snowman. Lightly press appliqué.

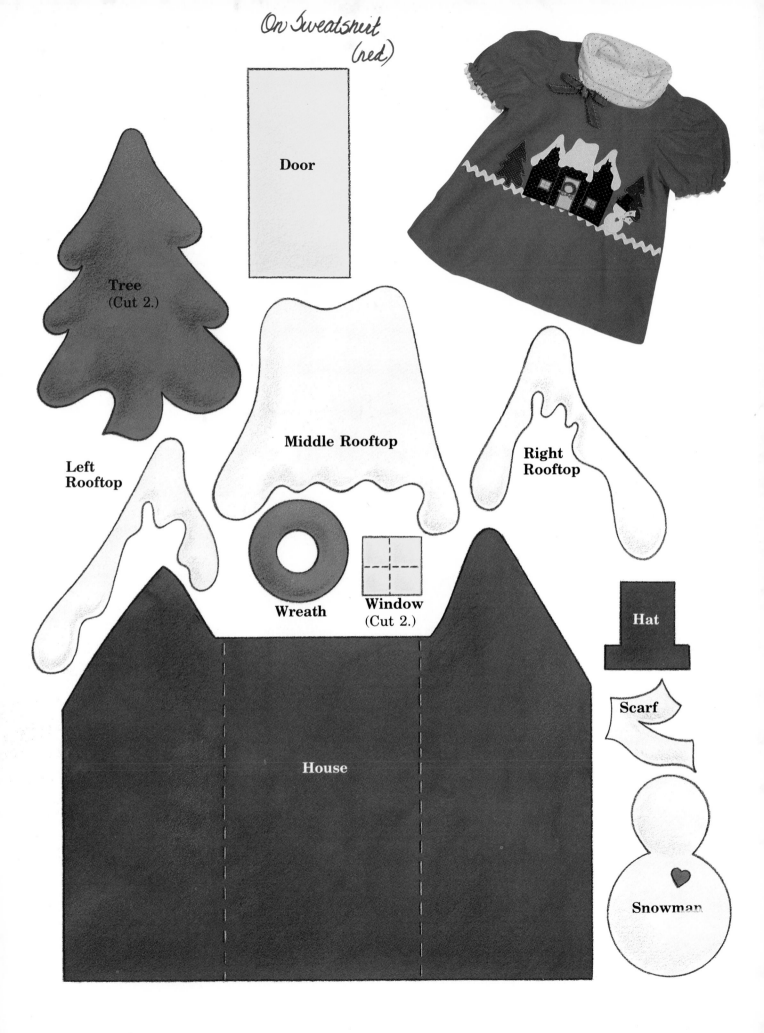

On Sweatshirt (red)

Door

Tree (Cut 2.)

Middle Rooftop

Left Rooftop

Right Rooftop

Wreath

Window (Cut 2.)

Hat

Scarf

House

Snowman

Mini-Mouse Scarf Set

Whee...! Following one simple graph, you can stitch the venturesome mouse appearing on this scarf, hat, and glove set, using one of two types of embroidery. Duplicate stitch may be used if there is a flat area on the knitted piece with at least 20 vertical and 17 horizontal stitches. If the knit stitches are too small or if the piece is woven and the weave is too difficult to follow, use waste canvas and cross-stitch the design.

You will need:

Scarf, hat, and gloves
Crewel needle
Lightweight yarn (gray, black, light pink,
and dark pink)
Silver metallic thread
Black embroidery floss
5 small pom-poms
1 extra-large pom-pom (for top of hat)
Waste canvas (for cross-stitch)

Duplicate Stitch

1. Match center of design to center of
piece being stitched. Count out from the
center of the design and place a straight
pin at all four outer limits to check design placement.

2. Thread needle with a 12″ strand of
yarn. Starting from the wrong side of the
piece, pull the needle up through the
stitch below the one to be covered, leaving about a 2″ tail of yarn. (Figure A.)
Pass the needle from right to left under
the stitch above the one to be covered.
(Figure A.) Reinsert the needle into the
stitch through which you originally pulled
the needle. (Figure B.)

3. Follow the graph and color key to
complete duplicate stitching, pulling your
stitches carefully so that the embroidery
covers the knitted stitches but does not
pucker the piece. When finished, weave
the end of the yarn through several
stitches on the wrong side of the piece.

4. Embroider the details, following the
graph and color key.

5. Securely tack a small pom-pom to the
tip of the mouse's hat. Sew the large pom-
pom to the top of the hat.

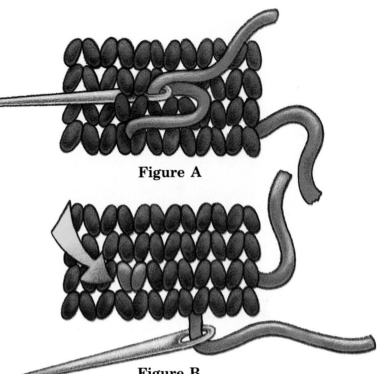

Figure A

Figure B

Cross-stitch

1. Cut waste canvas 1″ larger than the
design. Match centers of design and canvas. Center canvas on piece being
stitched; baste canvas in place.

2. Follow the graph and color key to
stitch the design.

3. Clip and remove the basting threads.
Dampen the waste canvas. Using tweez-
ers, carefully pull the canvas, thread by
thread, from under the stitches.

4. To finish, follow step 5 in the instructions for duplicate stitch.

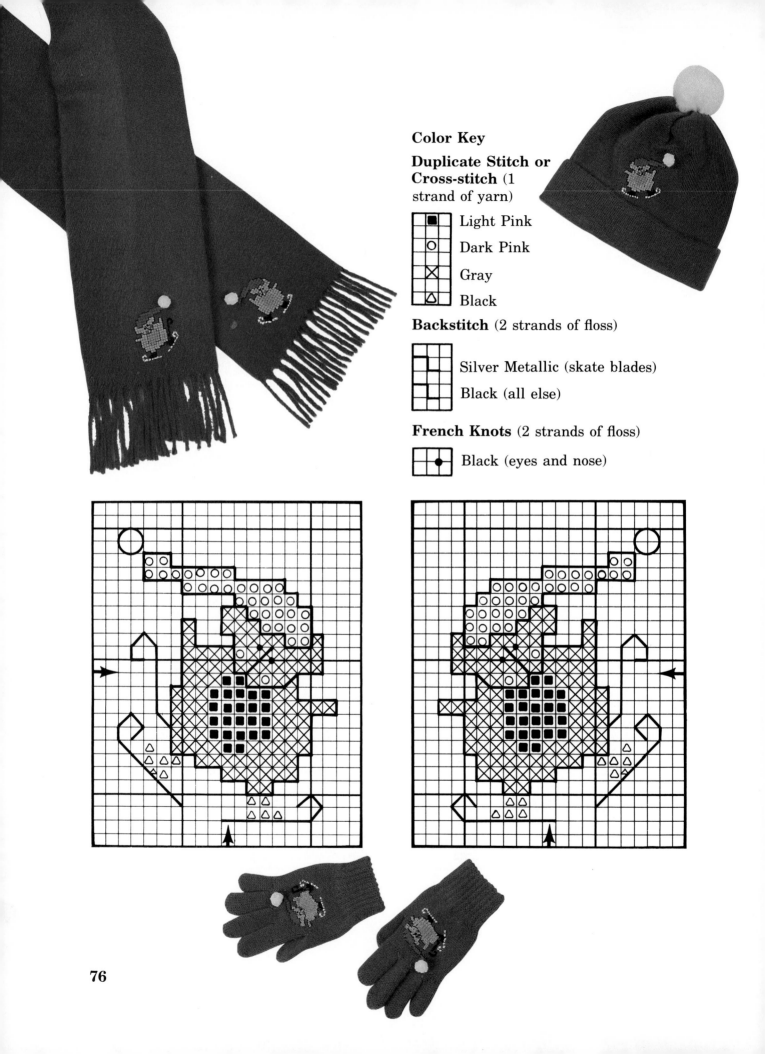

Color Key

Duplicate Stitch or Cross-stitch (1 strand of yarn)

■	Light Pink
O	Dark Pink
✕	Gray
△	Black

Backstitch (2 strands of floss)

Silver Metallic (skate blades)

Black (all else)

French Knots (2 strands of floss)

● Black (eyes and nose)

Super Socks

Here's a great gift for someone
you know with fun-loving feet!

Note: Before embellishing socks, desig-
nate a left one and a right one. Before
washing, turn socks so that buttons,
hearts, rosettes, and appliqués will be on
the inside. Dry flat.

Nifty Knee Socks
You will need:
1 pair of knee socks
½ yard (½″-wide) ribbon
6 pairs of novelty buttons

1. Fold down sock cuffs. Cut ribbon in
half and tie pieces into bows. Tack a bow
to each cuff, sewing through top layer
only. Trim ends of bows.

2. Sew buttons to socks, referring to
photograph for placement.

Ribbon Rosette Socks
You will need:

1 pair of crew socks
½ yard (1½"-wide) ribbon for rosettes
2 small heart buttons
¼ yard (½"-wide) ribbon for rosette trim

1. Cut the ribbon for the rosettes in half and sew the ends of each piece together, using ⅛" seam allowance. Using a double-knotted thread, hand-sew a row of gathering stitches down center of each ribbon. Pull ends of the threads to gather tightly, and knot securely. Fan out edges to make rosettes full.

2. Cut ribbon for trim in half. Fold each ribbon into a V and tack to back of a rosette. Trim ribbon ends at a slant. Sew button to center of each rosette.

3. Turn down cuffs on socks. Securely tack a ribbon rosette to each cuff, sewing through top layer only.

Sweetheart Socks
You will need:

1 pair of crew socks
2 (2½" x 5") pieces of fabric
2 (2½") squares of batting
1 yard (⅝"-wide) flat cluny lace
¼ yard (⅛"-wide) ribbon

1. To make each heart, fold piece of fabric with right sides together, forming a 2½" square. Using a sharp pencil, transfer heart pattern to fabric square. Place fabric square on top of one batting square and sew around entire heart. Trim heart, leaving ⅛" seam allowance. Carefully clip curves and point. Cut slit in heart for turning, cutting through only one layer of fabric. Turn heart right side out and press.

2. Cut lace in half. Stitch ends of each piece together, using ⅛" seam allowance. Lightly gather straight edge to fit around heart; knot thread securely. Baste gathered edge of lace to back of heart, spacing gathers evenly.

3. Cut ribbon in half and tie each piece into a bow. Tack bow to center top of heart. Turn down sock cuffs. Securely tack a heart to each cuff, stitching through top layer only.

Sweet Pea Socks
You will need:

1 pair of opaque white knee socks
Shirt cardboard
6 small heart buttons
Water-soluble marking pen
Paintbrush and acrylic paint
½ yard (⅜"-wide) ribbon

Pattern for Sweet Pea Socks

(Design shown is for right sock; reverse for left sock.)

1. Cut strips of cardboard and place them inside socks to absorb excess paint. Position buttons on socks. Using the marking pen, mark placement for the buttons; draw the leaves and flowers.

2. Paint the flowers with two coats of paint and let dry. Paint the vines and leaves. Allow paint to dry overnight. Set paint, using an iron (steam/wool setting) and pressing cloth.

3. Cut ribbon in half and tie the pieces into bows. Sew bows and buttons to socks. Trim ends of bows.

2. Cut two boat bottoms from blue fabric and two sails from dotted fabric. Set sewing machine for appliqué. Using satin stitch, appliqué boat bottom and sail to center of each felt square. Topstitch down center of sails. Cut tiny flag from white felt and glue to top of sail. Let dry. Trim appliqués, leaving 1/8″ border of red felt, and tack to socks.

3. Using two strands of floss, chain-stitch anchor chains on socks. Sew buttons to socks.

Pattern for Anchors Away Socks

(Design shown is for right sock; reverse for left sock.)

Anchors Away Socks
You will need:
1 pair of opaque white socks
Shirt cardboard
Water-soluble marking pen
Paintbrush and blue acrylic paint
Scraps of blue fabric, red-and-white
  polka-dot fabric, and white acrylic felt
Red and blue thread
2 (3″) squares of red acrylic felt
Craft glue
Embroidery needle and red floss
2 anchor buttons

1. Cut strips of cardboard and place inside socks to absorb excess paint. Draw waves with the marking pen. Paint waves with two coats of paint and let dry overnight. Set paint, using an iron (steam/wool setting) and pressing cloth.

Sunny Bunnies Sweatshirt

Who (save Mr. McGregor) wouldn't take a shine to these bright bunnies? Appliquéd, the big, flop-eared fellow stays put. Little Bunny, however, is stuffed and free to hop out of the shirt pocket and play!

You will need:
Sweatshirt
¼ yard (45"-wide) fabric
Contrasting and matching thread
¼ yard fusible web
Water-soluble marking pen
1 yard (1"-wide) ribbon
2 small buttons
Embroidery needle and floss
Polyester stuffing
½ yard (⅝"-wide) ribbon

Note: Use ¼" seam allow-ances throughout the project.

Big Bunny

1. Cut body and ear as marked. Using the marking pen, transfer features, including legs and toe lines, to fabric body.

2. Place fabric body on top of fusible web body and position on shirt. Fuse the pieces, following instructions of fusible web manufacturer.

3. Set machine for appliqué. Using contrasting thread and satin stitch, appliqué the body as follows: outline of body from point A up and over head to point B, as marked on pattern; toe lines and body outline between legs; legs. To ensure even coverage, satin-stitch again.

4. Cut the 1″-wide ribbon in half. Slightly gather end of one ribbon and pin to bunny's neck as marked on pattern; appliqué in place. Repeat for second ribbon.

5. With wrong sides together and leaving openings as marked, sew two ear pieces together. Clip curves; turn and press ears. Turn under raw edges ¼″ and blindstitch closed; gather edges slightly and sew to bunny head as marked on pattern. Repeat for second ear. Tack ears to shirt so that one stands and the other flops.

6. Using three strands of floss and satin stitch, embroider the nose and cheeks; use backstitch for the mouth. Sew button eyes in place. Tie neck ribbons into a bow and trim the ends.

Pocket and Little Bunny

1. Transfer patterns to fabric and cut as marked. Transfer pleat markings to pocket.

2. Turn under top edge of pocket ¼″ and press; turn under edge ½″ and blindstitch. To make pleats, on right side, bring dotted lines to dotted lines in direction of arrow. Pin; press and baste. Position pocket on shirt and baste; tack pleats at top edge of pocket. Satin-stitch side and bottom edges of pocket, leaving top edge open; satin-stitch edges again.

3. Sew legs and ears with wrong sides together, leaving openings as marked. Clip curves; turn and press pieces. Firmly stuff legs to within 1″ of tops.

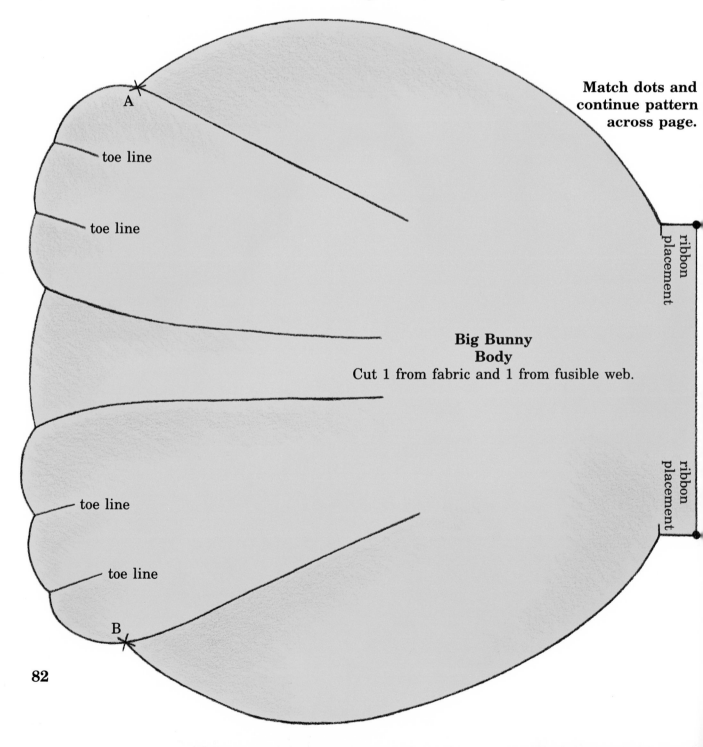

A

toe line

toe line

Match dots and continue pattern across page.

ribbon placement

Big Bunny Body
Cut 1 from fabric and 1 from fusible web.

ribbon placement

toe line

toe line

B

Slightly gather raw edges of ears and pin to right side of head front as marked, aligning raw edges; machine-baste. Pin legs to right side of body front as marked, aligning raw edges, and baste. With right sides together, sew bottom edge of head front to top edge of body front.

4. With right sides together, sew body front to body back, keeping ears and legs away from seam and leaving opening as marked. Clip curves. Turn and press bunny; stuff firmly. Turn under edges of opening and blindstitch closed.

Patterns for Big Bunny

5. Embroider the face, using three strands of floss and the following stitches: satin stitch for cheeks and nose, French knots (three wraps) for eyes, and backstitch for mouth. Tie ribbon around bunny's neck and make a bow.

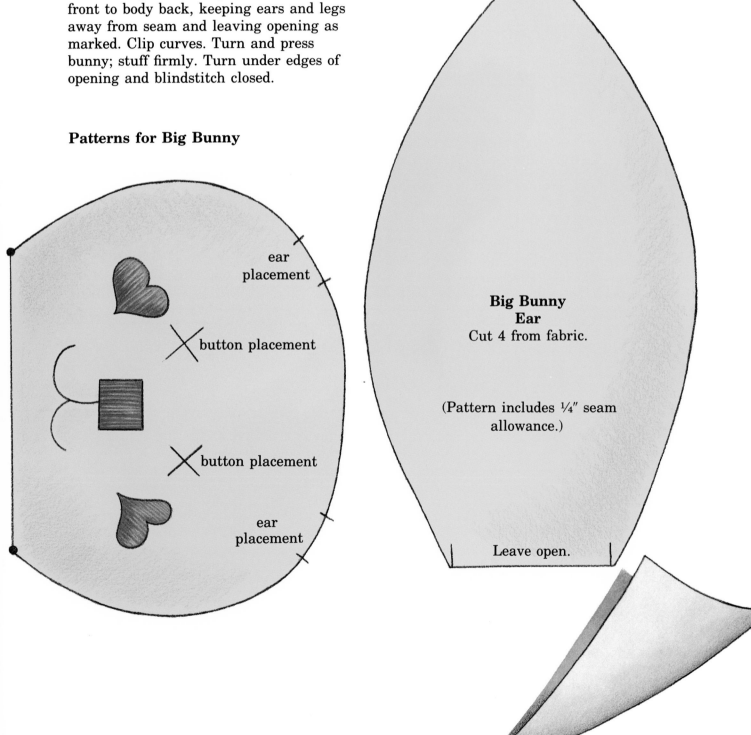

ear placement

✕ button placement

button placement

ear placement

**Big Bunny
Ear**
Cut 4 from fabric.

(Pattern includes ¼″ seam allowance.)

Leave open.

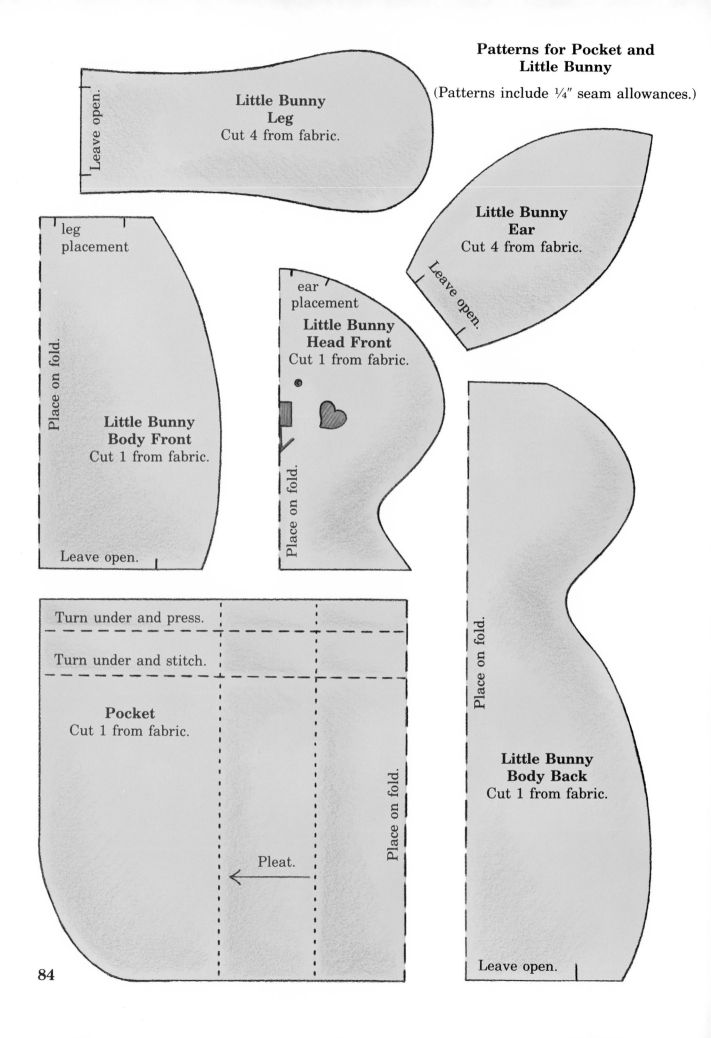

Little Bunny Leg
Cut 4 from fabric.

Leave open.

Little Bunny Ear
Cut 4 from fabric.

Leave open.

leg placement

Place on fold.

Little Bunny Body Front
Cut 1 from fabric.

Leave open.

ear placement

Little Bunny Head Front
Cut 1 from fabric.

Place on fold.

Place on fold.

Little Bunny Body Back
Cut 1 from fabric.

Turn under and press.

Turn under and stitch.

Pocket
Cut 1 from fabric.

Place on fold.

Pleat.

84

Leave open.

Holiday Sweater

Turn a plain-Jane sweater into a festive favorite with ribbon-trimmed eyelet, bells, buttons, and bows.

Note: This sweater is not recommended for children under three years of age.

You will need (for small cardigan):
2 yards (½″-wide) ribbon
2 yards (1″-wide) gathered eyelet trim
Novelty buttons, jingle bells, and bows

1. With edges aligned, sew ribbon to eyelet. Cut eyelet bands to fit around armhole seams and bottom ribbing, allowing ¼″ extra for turning under ends. Starting at underarm seam, hand-baste bands around armhole seams; machine-baste band along top edge of ribbing. Machine-stitch bands to sweater, sewing along ribbon edges.

2. Replace original buttons with novelty buttons. Arrange remaining buttons, bells, and bows on sweater; tape in place. Sew securely.

3. To machine-wash sweater, button it, turn it inside out, and enclose it in a pillowcase. Launder as usual.

Dinosuit

Some say they went out long ago. But ask any youngster what's "in" these days, and he'll answer—dinosaurs!

Not a project to be completed quickly, this one requires appliquéing, stenciling, and strip piecing. The results are unique and well worth the effort, but don't hesitate to omit the arm and leg bands if you're short on expertise or time. (A plain suit bearing this handsome beast will still stand out in a crowd!)

You will need:

Sweat suit

¼ yard paper-backed fusible web

9″ x 16″ piece of green fabric

¼ yard (45″-wide) yellow fabric

⅛ yard (36″-wide) each of white, red, and blue fabric

Thread to match

Lightweight paper (for point pattern and for stabilizing appliqué)

½ yard (¹⁄₁₆″-wide) black ribbon

Embroidery needle

White and black embroidery floss

1 small pom-pom

3″ x 9″ piece of stencil plastic

Craft knife

Stencil brush

Black stencil paint

Note: Use ¼″ seam allowances throughout the project.

Appliqué

1. Cut a 9″ x 16″ piece of web; trace pattern for dinosaur onto paper side. On scraps of web, trace hat, toe (six times), and balloon (two times). Referring to photograph for color of fabrics, cut pieces of fabric large enough to back web pieces. Following manufacturer's instructions, fuse web pieces to fabric pieces. Trim fabrics to match web.

2. Trace and cut out point pattern. To make points, cut two 2½″ x 40″ strips of yellow fabric. Fold each strip with long edges and wrong sides together and press; cut folded strips into 2½″ pieces. Center point pattern on top of one 2½″ piece and fold piece as shown. Slide pattern out. Press point and pin to secure; turn point over and trim excess along bottom edge. Connect points by machine-basting them together, stitching ¼″ from bottom edge of points and taking one or two stitches between each point. (Be sure last fold is caught in basting.)

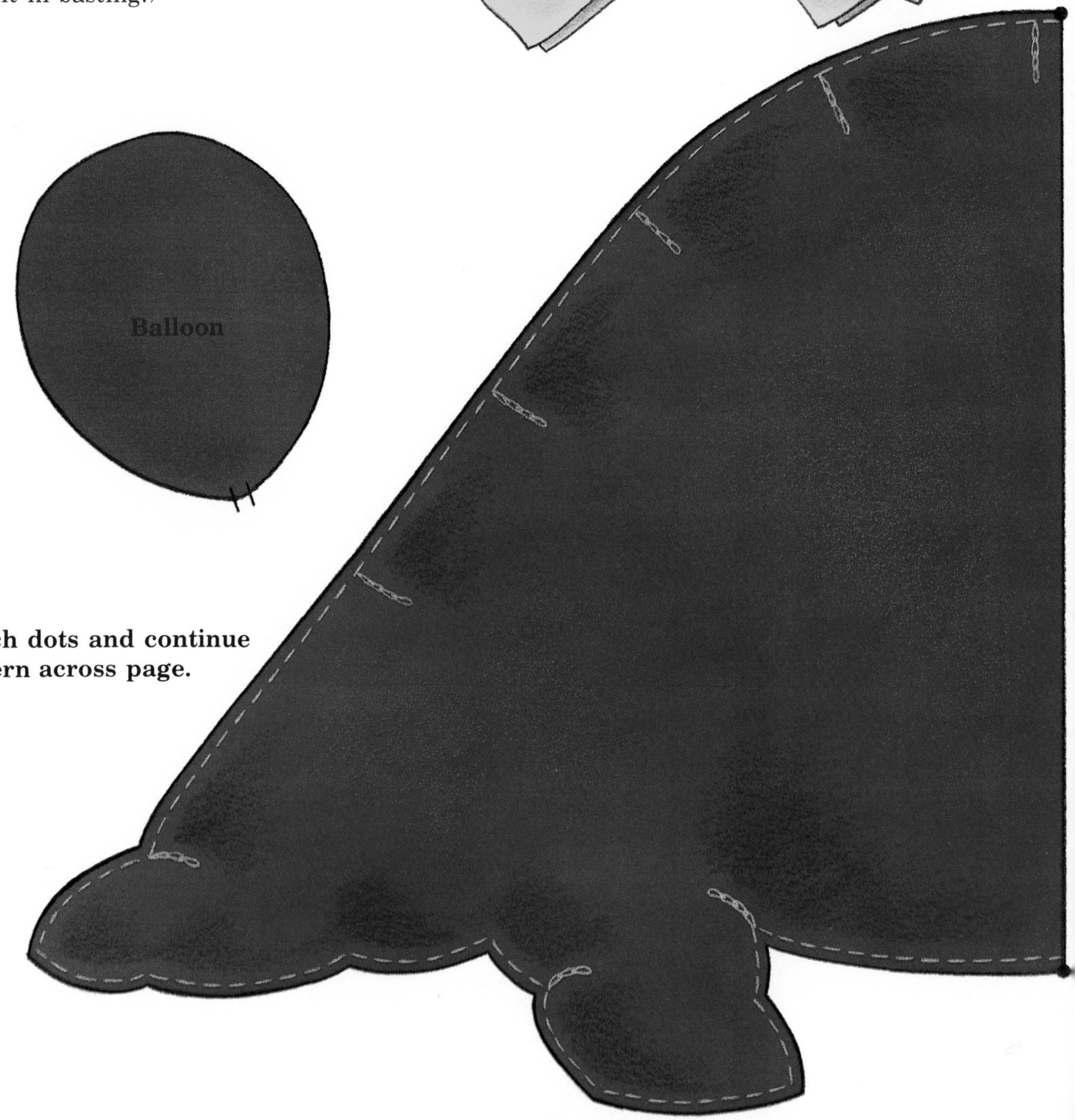

Balloon

Match dots and continue pattern across page.

88

3. Remove paper backing from dinosaur. Position dinosaur on sweatshirt and press very lightly with iron. Repeat for remaining pieces. Cut off nine connected points. Gently lift edge of dinosaur's back and position points; cut ribbon in half and position ends under edges of balloons. Following manufacturer's instructions, fuse the appliqué pieces.

4. Cut two pieces of lightweight paper, one large enough to back dinosaur and one to back balloons; pin paper pieces to inside of shirt. Set machine for appliqué.

Using matching thread, appliqué the pieces to the shirt. Tear away paper from inside shirt. Press appliqué. Using white thread and regular stitch, topstitch dinosaur as marked on pattern.

5. Using one strand of black floss and outline stitch, embroider toes inside stitching. Using three strands of black floss, make French knot for nose; satin-stitch eye and backstitch mouth. Using three strands of white floss, satin-stitch cheek; backstitch "crease" lines. Sew pompom to hat. Tie loose ribbon ends into bow and tack bow to dinosaur point; trim ends of bow.

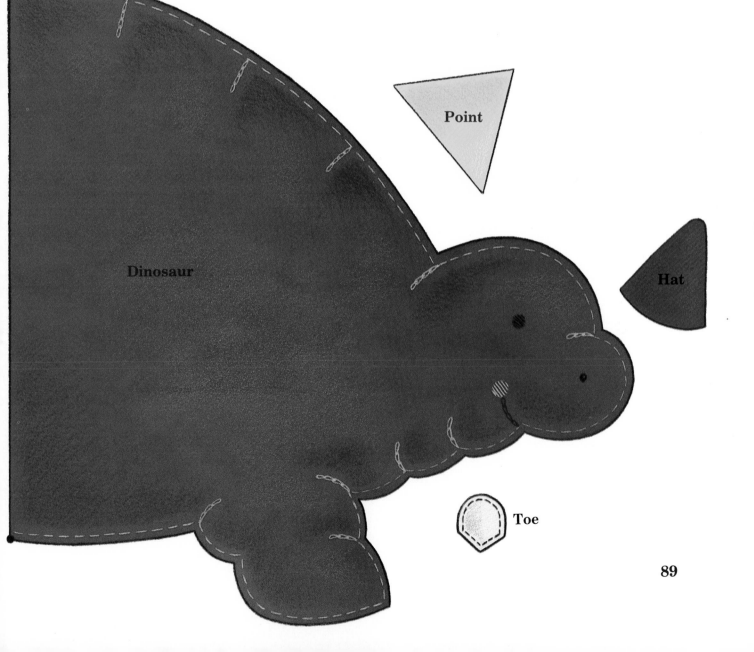

Point

Dinosaur

Hat

Toe

Strip Piecing and Stenciling

1. Cut a 3¾″-wide band of material from right shirtsleeve and left pant leg. Open seams by removing stitches. Measure top edge of sleeve band and add 1″. Using this measurement for length, cut one 2¼″-wide strip from white fabric, one 1¼″-wide strip from blue fabric, and one 1¼″-wide strip from red fabric. Cut strips for pant leg in same manner.

2. Cut stencil for footprints. Stencil footprints on white fabric strips. (For special effect, use drier brush for "pads" than for toes.) Let paint dry overnight. To set footprints, press for 15 to 20 seconds, using pressing cloth and very hot, dry iron.

3. Place band cut from shirt with right side and top edge up. Place red fabric strip, right side up, along bottom edge of band and machine-baste strip to band. With right sides together and edges aligned, sew stenciled strip to red strip, stitching through all three layers. Turn stenciled strip right side up and press lightly. With right sides together and raw edges aligned, sew blue strip to stenciled strip. Turn blue strip right side up and press lightly; machine-baste top edge to band. Sew strips to pant band in same manner. Trim excess fabric from strips. With right sides together, sew ends of bands back together. Finish seams with zigzag or overlock stitch.

4. Cut a string of points to fit around cut edge on shirt. With points facing up, machine-baste bottom edges of points to shirt edge. (Hold connecting threads tightly while basting points.) Cut string of points for pant leg and sew in same manner.

5. With right sides together and seams aligned, sew band to shirt sleeve. (Be sure to catch bottom edges of points in seam.) With right sides together and seams aligned, sew bottom portion of sleeve to band. Re-attach band to pant leg in same manner. Finish seams with zigzag or overlock stitch. To make points stand up, turn seam allowance toward band and whipstitch. Turn shirt and pants right side out and press.

Footprints

Knit Picks

Cute and colorful, these hand-knit sweaters are bound to be favorites with kids. A chocolate sundae, topped with whipped cream and a pom-pom cherry, sweetens her hot-pink pullover vest. Long-sleeved, his sky-blue sweater sports a fanciful plane, soaring through puffy white clouds.

You will need:

#4 and #8 knitting needles
#4 circular knitting needle
Bobbins (optional)
Stitch holder
Tapestry needle

For the **Sundae Sweater Vest:** 4
(50-gram) skeins hot pink for sizes
small and medium, or 5 (50-gram)
skeins hot pink for size large; 1
(50-gram) skein vanilla; 1 (50-gram)
skein blue-green; small amount of
brown for fudge sauce; small amount of
white for whipped cream (Vendome
Maxime yarn used in model for
texture); red pom-pom for cherry

For the **Airplane Sweater:** 6 (50-gram)
skeins blue for sizes small and medium,
or 8 (50-gram) skeins blue for size
large; 1 (50-gram) skein red; 1
(50-gram) skein yellow; 1 (50-gram)
skein white; small amount of
blue-green for pilot's helmet; small
amount of black for goggles and
propeller

Standard Knitting Abbreviations

st(s)—stitch(es)   **beg**—begin(ning)
K—knit   **dec**—decrease(s)
P—purl   **inc**—increase(s)
St st—stockinette stitch **rem**—remain(ing)

Sizing Chart	S	M	L
Chest (actual)	23″	24″	26″
Chest (finished)	25½″	26½″	28½″
Length (shoulder to hip)	17″	17½″	18½″
Sleeve length	10½″	11¾″	13″

Gauge: 4½ sts = 1″; 6 rows St st = 1″ on
larger needles. Work a sample on suggested size needles to check your tension
before beginning the project. If your
swatch is too tight, change to larger needles; if too loose, change to smaller needles. It is imperative for proper fit that
your gauge be as directed.

Note: Since it is best not to carry thread
over more than two stitches, it may be
easier to wind yarn on bobbins while
working the graph. To avoid holes, twist
old yarn over new when changing colors.
Directions are given for size small. Directions for sizes medium and large are in
parentheses.

Sundae Sweater Vest:

Back: With smaller needles and hot pink,
cast on 59 (61, 65) sts. Work in P 1, K 1
ribbing as follows: 3 rows hot pink, 2
rows blue-green, 4 rows hot pink, 2 rows
vanilla, 4 rows hot pink, 2 rows blue-
green, 2 rows hot pink. Change to larger
needles and work St st in hot pink until
piece measures 17″ (17½″, 18½″) from beg.
Bind off loosely.

Front: Work ribbing as for back. Change
to larger needles and work St st in hot
pink for 5 (6, 9) rows before beg graph.
Follow graph for proper size and change
colors as indicated. When piece measures
14½″ (15″, 16″) from beg, shape neckline
(graph should be completed).

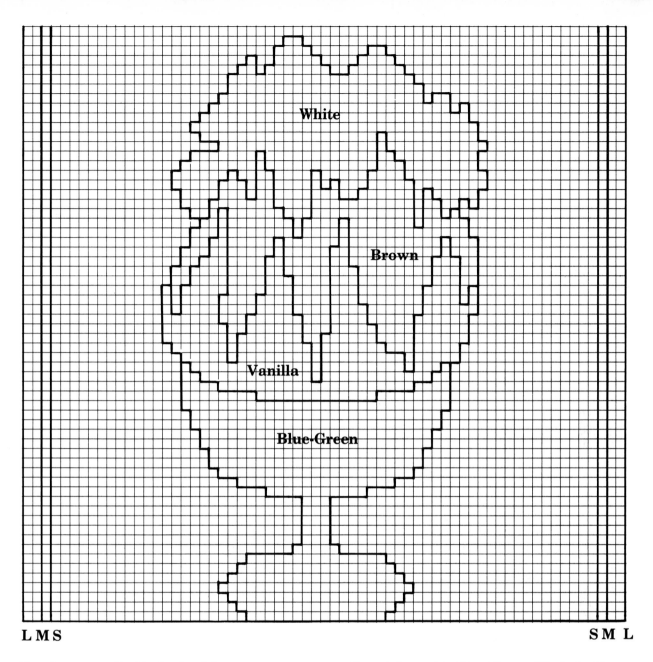

L M S   **S M L**

To shape neck: Both shoulders are worked at the same time, using separate yarn. With hot pink, work across 21 (22, 23) sts, slip the center 17 (17, 19) sts to a stitch holder, attach another skein of hot pink and work across 21 (22, 23) rem sts. Continue working in St st, dec 1 st each side of neck edge every other row, 4 times. Work even on 17 (18, 19) sts for each shoulder until piece measures 17″ (17½″, 18½″) from beg, or same as back. Bind off each shoulder loosely.

To finish: Using tapestry needle and matching yarn, weave shoulder seams. For neck, with hot pink and circular nee-dle, pick up 72 (72, 78) sts. Work in K 1, P 1 ribbing in the round as follows: 1 row each of blue-green, hot pink, vanilla, blue-green, hot pink. Then bind off loosely in ribbing with hot pink. For arm-hole, measure down side seams from shoulder seam 6¾″ (7″, 7½″) and mark this point on front and back pieces. Be-tween these marks, pick up in hot pink 58 (60, 64) sts. Work in P 1, K 1 ribbing in same color sequence as for neck. Bind off loosely in ribbing with hot pink. Weave side seam from bottom to under-arm. Attach red pom-pom to the top of the sundae with a small safety pin.

Airplane Sweater:

Back: With smaller needles and blue, cast on 59 (61, 65) sts. Work in P 1, K 1 ribbing as follows: 1 row blue, 2 rows red, 2 rows blue, 2 rows yellow, 2 rows blue, 2 rows red, 2 rows blue, 2 rows white, 2 rows blue. Change to larger needles and work in St st in blue until piece measures 17″ (17½″, 18½″) from beg. Bind off loosely.

Front: Work ribbing as for back. Change to larger needles and work in St st in blue yarn for 3 (4, 7) rows before beg graph. Follow graph for proper size and change colors as indicated. When piece measures 14½″ (15″, 16″) from beg, shape neckline (graph should be completed).

To shape neck: Both shoulders are worked at the same time, using separate yarn. With blue, work across 21 (22, 23)

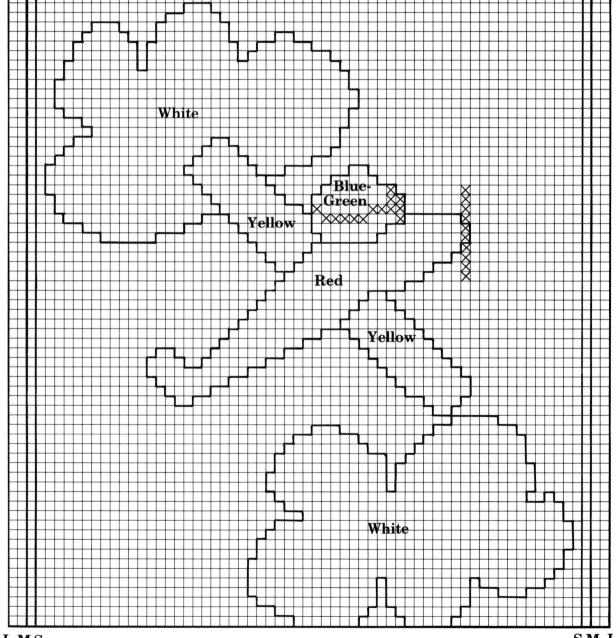

L M S   S M L

sts, slip the center 17 (17, 19) sts to a stitch holder, attach another skein of blue and work across 21 (22, 23) rem sts. Continue working in St st, dec 1 st each side of neck edge every other row 4 times. Work even on 17 (18, 19) sts for each shoulder until piece measures 17″ (17½″, 18½″) from beg or same as back. Bind off each shoulder loosely.

Sleeves: With smaller needles and blue, cast on 29 (31, 33) sts. Work in P 1, K 1 ribbing in same color sequence as ribbing at waist of sweater. Change to larger needles and inc 5 sts evenly across the first row of St st. When sleeve measures 3″ from beg, inc 1 st each end of needle, every ¾″, 10 times, until 54 (56, 58) sts are on needle. Work even until piece measures 10½″ (11¾″, 13″) from beg. Bind off loosely.

To finish: Using tapestry needle and matching yarn, weave shoulder seams. For neck, with blue and circular needle, pick up 72 (72, 78) sts. Work in K 1, P 1 ribbing in the round as follows: 1 row each of blue, white, blue, red, blue, yellow, blue. Then bind off loosely in ribbing with blue. For sleeves, measure down side seams from shoulder seam 6¾″ (7″, 7½″) and mark this point on front and back pieces. Match center top of sleeve to shoulder seam. Weave sleeve to sweater body. Weave sleeve seam from wrist to underarm. Weave sweater side seam from bottom to underarm. With tapestry needle and black, duplicate-stitch goggles and propeller, as indicated on graph.

Suite Dreams

A-Door-a-Bells

Ding-a-ling! Not just jumping jacks, these plump wooden teddies are bedroom doorbell ringers!

You will need (for each bear):
6″ x 12″ (⅛″) best-grade plywood
Band saw (or scroll saw)
Electric drill with ³⁄₃₂″ and ⁹⁄₆₄″ bits
Sandpaper
Paintbrush (½″ wide)
Stencil paint (including white, tan, and pink)
Stencil brush
Stencil plastic
Black fine-tip pen
Craft knife
Masking tape
Hot glue gun
½″ letters (transfer art)
1 yard (⅛″) cording
6½″ (⅛″) wood doweling
8 natural-color round beads with ⅛″ holes (for assembly)
1 small jingle bell
1 (2″-long) sawtooth picture hanger
3 beads with ⅛″ holes (for pull)
For **Girl:** 6″ x 10″ piece of netting, 3¾″ (⅜″-wide) flat lace, 1 yard (⅛″-wide) satin ribbon, 3¾″ string of #3 craft pearls, 4 ribbon roses (purchased)
For **Boy:** stencil paint and fine-tip pen for vest, 1¼″ (¾″-wide) craft ribbon, ⅓ yard (⅛″-wide) satin ribbon, scrap of felt

Cutting Out and Painting the Bear

1. Transfer patterns (outline only) for body, arms, legs, and heart (girl only) to plywood; cut pieces as marked, using the band saw. Mark placement for holes. Drill holes, using the ³⁄₃₂″ bit for the small holes and the ⁹⁄₆₄″ bit for the large holes. Sand all surfaces smooth.

3. Using fine-tip pen, trace pattern for face stencil, including outline, onto small piece of plastic. Place tracing on an old magazine or a piece of thick cardboard. Using the knife, cut openings for ears, nose, and cheeks. Position stencil on face and lightly tape edges. Using pink paint and stencil brush, stencil features (and dab paint on heart), applying several light coats of paint and letting paint dry between coats. Remove stencil. Let dry.

4. Transfer eyes, mouth, and paw pads to wood pieces. Using black pen, color the features; outline the nose. Add eyelashes to girl bear.

Dressing the Bear

1. For **Girl,** run tape across body 2″ from bottom edge, to provide guideline for letters. Following manufacturer's instructions, apply the letters above the tape; remove tape.

2. Cut a 6″ x 8″ piece of netting and a 3¾″ piece of ribbon. Fold netting in half with long edges together; fold again (to make 1½″ x 8″ piece). Gather top edge with a running stitch and adjust to fit body; secure threads. Glue gathered edge to body, ¼″ below letters, pressing so that all layers adhere. Glue lace, ribbon, and pearls along gathered edge. Seal ends of pearls with tiny dots of glue. Let dry.

3. Cut a 1″ square of netting and gather one side to make a fan; glue fan to head as marked. Cut ribbon pieces for feet and glue in place. Glue roses to fan and feet. Let dry.

4. For **Boy,** trace pattern for vest stencil on small piece of plastic; following outline, cut stencil. Position stencil on body, centering the V-neck. Using stencil brush and paint, stencil the vest. Let dry. Out-

2. Using the   paintbrush and white stencil paint,   apply base coat to all surfaces. Let   dry. Dip stencil brush in tan paint   and dab on scrap paper to remove excess. Using very dry brush and an up-and-down motion, dab paint on body, arm, and leg pieces. (Apply more paint to edges than centers, keeping overall coverage light.) Let dry.

Figure A

line top and bottom edges with pen; draw ribbing lines as marked on pattern.

5. Following manufacturer's instructions and noting curve of vest, apply letters ⅜″ above bottom edge of vest.

6. To make bow tie, gather craft ribbon at center; secure threads. Glue a tiny piece of ribbon around center of bow. Glue tie in place. Let dry.

Assembling the Bear

1. For **Girl,** cut four 4″ pieces of cording and four ⅝″ pieces of doweling. Pull a piece of cording through small hole on arm and tie a knot at the edge. (Figure A.) Repeat for remaining arm and legs. Lay body face down. Lay arms and legs face down on body, aligning large holes. Insert a dowel in each hole and position so that exposed ends are equal lengths. Using a toothpick apply glue to ends of one dowel; slip round beads onto ends. Quickly check to see if limb moves freely; adjust beads if necessary. Repeat for remaining dowels. Let dry.

2. Trim remaining dowel to 3½″. Cut a 1″ x 2″ piece of netting, a 4½″ piece of ribbon, and a 6″ piece of ribbon. Glue heart along top ¾″ of dowel. Let dry. Gather netting at center to make a bow; fold bow to make a fan and glue to dowel, beneath heart. Thread bell onto one end of the 6″ ribbon; knot ribbon to secure bell. Glue other end of ribbon around dowel, over netting. Make a bow with the 4½″ ribbon and glue to bottom of heart; glue rose onto bow. Glue wand to back of paw at an angle. Let dry.

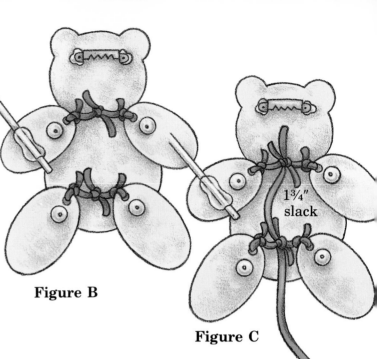

Figure B

Figure C

3. Center hanger on back of bear head, ¾″ from top, and glue securely. Let dry. With bear face down, position arms and legs in resting position as shown. (Figure B.) Tie ends of both arm cords together in a knot, making sure paw pads will show from front. Tie and knot ends of both leg cords, making sure knot does not extend below body when pulled. For pull, tie remaining piece of cording in knot around the arm knot; leaving 1¾″ of slack, tie pull in a knot around leg knot. (Figure C.) Gently tug on pull to check movement; make adjustments if necessary. Trim pull to 9″ (from bottom edge of body). Thread beads onto pull; knot end. Trim remaining cord ends to ¼″ or more. Secure knots with glue. Let dry.

4. For **Boy,** assemble same as for Girl, step 1.

5. Cut flag from felt and glue around end of remaining dowel. Tie bell onto end of a 6″ piece of ribbon; secure with a knot. Glue other end of ribbon around dowel, below the flag. Fold a 1½″ piece of ribbon into a V and glue over the glued ribbon end. Glue dowel to back of paw at an angle. Let dry.

6. Assemble same as for Girl, step 3.

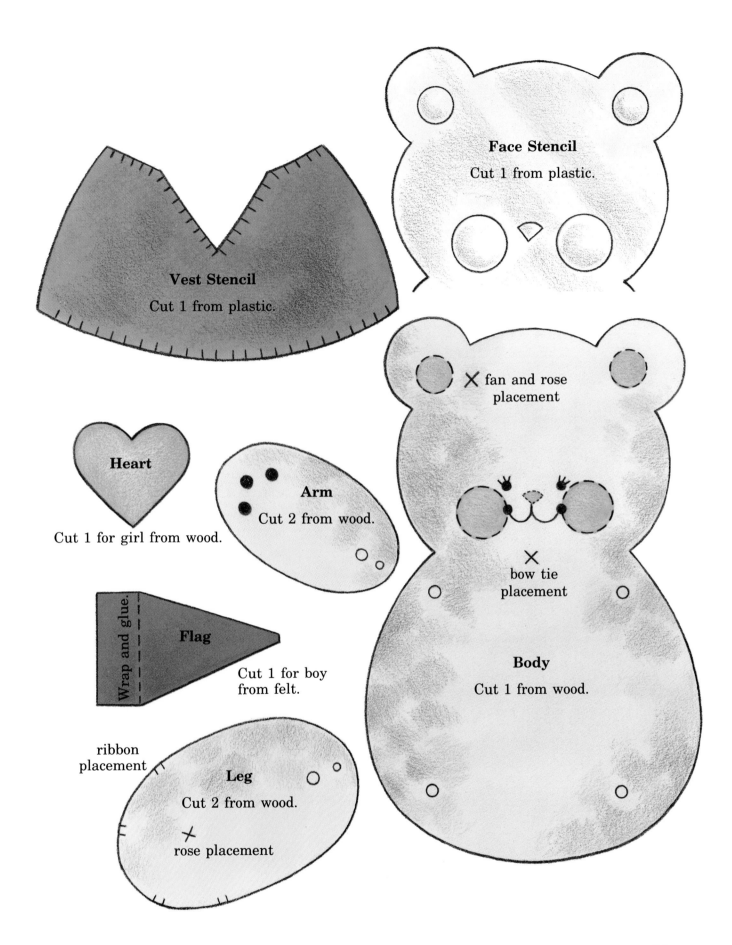

Vest Stencil

Cut 1 from plastic.

Face Stencil

Cut 1 from plastic.

Heart

Cut 1 for girl from wood.

Arm

Cut 2 from wood.

✕ fan and rose
placement

bow tie
placement

Flag

Wrap and glue.

Cut 1 for boy
from felt.

ribbon
placement

Leg

Cut 2 from wood.

✕
rose placement

Body

Cut 1 from wood.

Moon Bunnies Quilt

In luscious shades of yellow and blue, this dreamy quilt will grace a nursery wall, rest sweetly upon a bed, or keep friends cozy while they read a book.

You will need:
1¾ yards (45″-wide) yellow chintz
¼ yard of bleached muslin
Small scrap of green chintz
1 yard (45″-wide) blue cotton fabric
⅓ yard fusible web
1¼ yards of fleece
Water-soluble marking pen
Thread to match fabrics
Embroidery, crewel, and quilting needles
Blue and pink embroidery floss
7 to 8 yards each of fancy white and
    fancy green yarn (fingering weight)
Quilting hoop
White and brown quilting thread
35½″ x 43″ piece of batting

Note: All quilting is by hand. Approximate finished size of quilt is 35″ x 42½″.

1. Cut pieces for appliqué as marked, cutting fabric and web pieces simultaneously. Cut one 35½″ x 43″ rectangle (for quilt top) from blue fabric and one 43½″ x 51″ rectangle (for quilt backing) from yellow chintz. From fleece, cut two 3½″ x 43″ strips and two 3½″ x 32″ strips. Mark features on bunnies, using the marking pen.

2. With fabric pieces (right side up) on top of fusible web pieces, position moon and stars on quilt top; pin. Following instructions of fusible web manufacturer, fuse the pieces. Pin and fuse carrot and bunny pieces in same manner.

3. Set machine for appliqué. Using matching thread and satin stitch, appliqué pieces in the following order: moon, stars, carrot, sitting bunnies, hopping bunny; appliqué bunny tails. Using three strands of blue floss and embroidery needle, satin-stitch bunnies' eyes; satin-stitch heart cheeks with three strands of pink floss. Sew star and carrot strings, as instructed on placement diagram, using crewel needle and white yarn.

4. Using the marking pen and referring to diagram for placement, transfer the hearts and stars to the quilt top; draw furrows. Place quilt backing wrong side up. Center batting and then quilt top (right side up) on backing. Hand-baste together in a 5″ grid.

5. Using the hoop, quilting needle, and white thread, quilt ¼″ outside the appliquéd pieces; quilt bunny legs and ears as shown in diagram. Using brown thread, quilt the furrows. Quilt remaining stars and the hearts with white thread.

6. To make binding, fold the fleece strips in half with long edges together. Align edges of fleece strips and quilt top, and pin. (Fleece fold is toward center of quilt.) Bring backing over fleece, tucking ½″ of backing under fleece fold. Slipstitch backing to quilt top, mitering the corners. Using white thread, outline quilt top (blue),¼″ in from edge of binding.

7. For the carrot-top bows, cut twenty-nine 9″ pieces of green yarn. Fold each piece of yarn in half three times and tack the center to the quilt as marked.

8. For each sitting bunny's tail, wrap white yarn 50 times around a ½″-wide strip of cardboard. At one end of the looped yarn, slip a piece of yarn through the loops and tie; cut the loops at the other end. Make the hopping bunny's tail in the same manner, wrapping white yarn 100 times around a 1″-wide strip of cardboard. Securely tack pom-pom tails to centers of appliquéd tails.

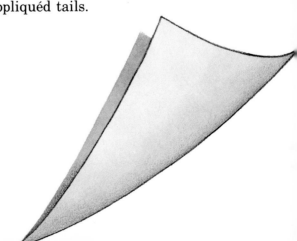

Quilting and Placement Diagram

Broken lines indicate quilting lines.

Leave ends of strings free and longer than necessary. After quilting has been completed, couch strings (through quilt top only) to secure. Trim ends of strings.

Start strings (knotted) at points shown on stars and carrot top, entering from back of quilt top.

Use star patterns on facing page for quilting patterns.

15½"

17¼"

6¼"

5¾"

Numbers indicate distance of furrows from bottom edge of quilt top.

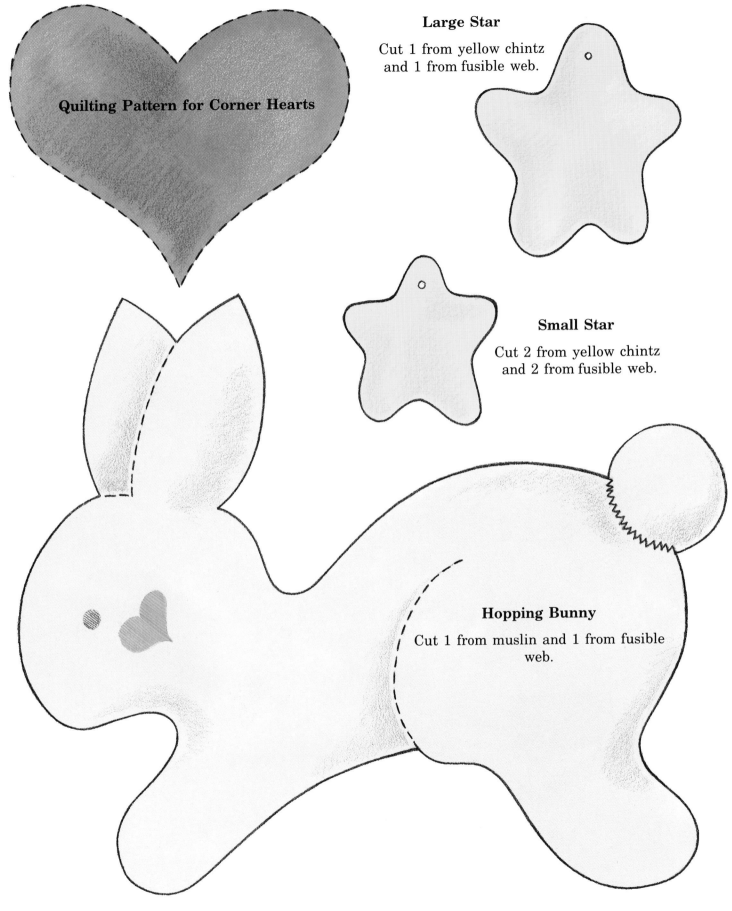

Quilting Pattern for Corner Hearts

Large Star

Cut 1 from yellow chintz
and 1 from fusible web.

Small Star

Cut 2 from yellow chintz
and 2 from fusible web.

Hopping Bunny

Cut 1 from muslin and 1 from fusible
web.

103

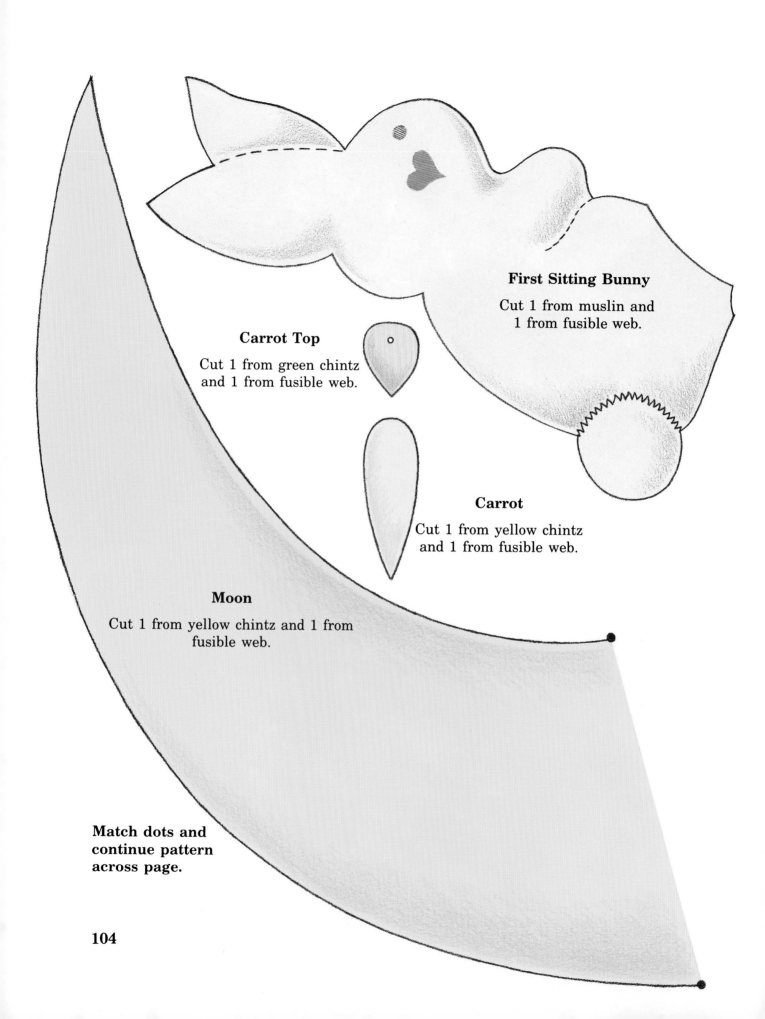

First Sitting Bunny

Cut 1 from muslin and
1 from fusible web.

Carrot Top

Cut 1 from green chintz
and 1 from fusible web.

Carrot

Cut 1 from yellow chintz
and 1 from fusible web.

Moon

Cut 1 from yellow chintz and 1 from
fusible web.

**Match dots and
continue pattern
across page.**

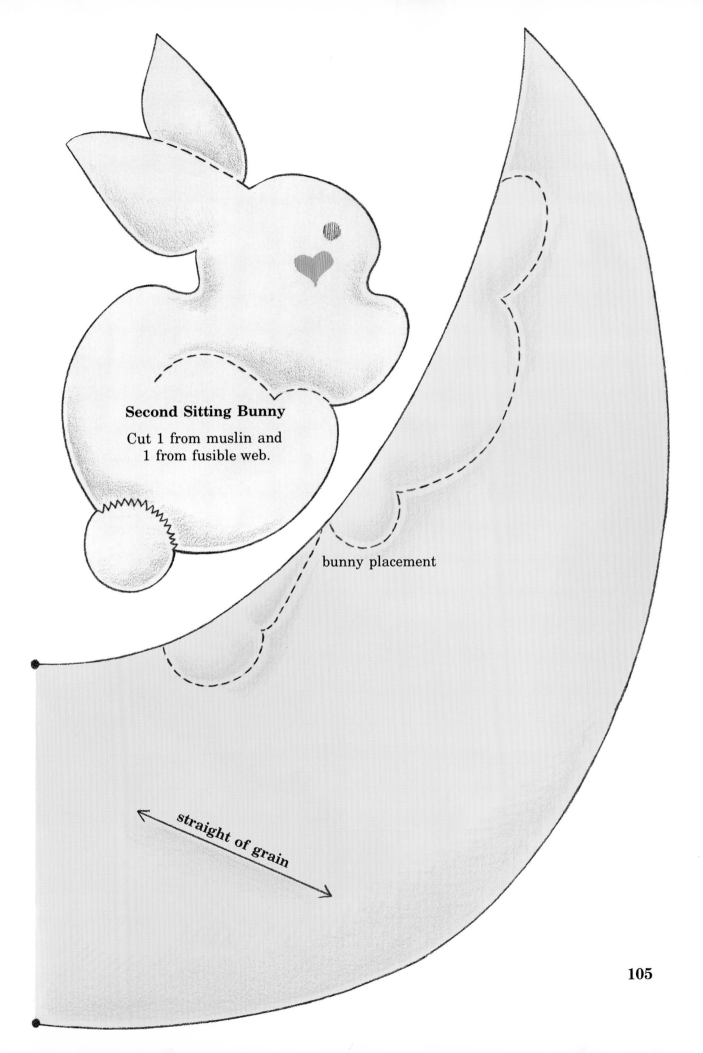

Second Sitting Bunny

Cut 1 from muslin and
1 from fusible web.

bunny placement

straight of grain

Kitty Caddy

A contented kitty takes a snooze, evidently unaware that her lunch is passing by!

Made for a bedside, the striped portion of this cleverly designed caddy fits under the mattress. The eyelet-trimmed pockets will hold paper and pens, scissors, small books, and other items that are nice to have at hand.

You will need:

⅞ yard (36″-wide) blue-striped fabric
½ yard (45″-wide) peach pindot fabric
4″ x 5″ piece of yellow corduroy
⅓ yard (45″-wide) medium-weight robe velour
7″ x 16″ piece of print fabric (for bow)
Thread to match fabrics and ribbon
Water-soluble marking pen
½ yard (45″-wide) thin batting
¼ yard medium-weight interfacing
4″ x 5″ piece of paper-backed web
1¾ yards yellow bias tape (single fold)
1¾ yards (¼″) cording
⅓ yard (⅛″-wide) yellow satin ribbon
Embroidery needle and floss (blue, peach, and yellow)
16″ (1″-wide) gathered eyelet trim
⅓ yard (⅜″-wide) flat lace
Scraps of 1″-wide yellow and peach satin ribbon
5″ (⅛″-wide) blue satin ribbon

Note: Use ¼″ seam allowances throughout project unless instructed otherwise.

Mattress Flap

1. To make pattern for flap, cut a 13¾″ x 26″ paper rectangle. Trace pattern for large pocket and cut out full size; mark dots and placement for pleats. Fold pocket pattern on center line, right sides together. Starting at bottom of pleat mark, run a line of pins (parallel with center line) to top of pocket. Open pattern. With bottom edges aligned, center pattern on one end of paper rectangle; trim sides of rectangle to match sides of pocket. Fold flap pattern with long edges together and round off top corners to complete flap pattern. (See figure.)

2. Cut two flap pieces from striped fabric and one from batting. Transfer dots to right side of one flap piece, as indicated. (See figure.) This will be flap front. Remove pins from pocket pattern.

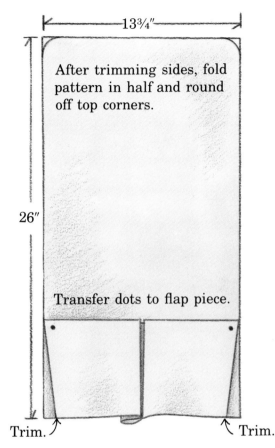

13¾″

26″

After trimming sides, fold pattern in half and round off top corners.

Transfer dots to flap piece.

Trim.　　　　Trim.

3. Cut one 56″ piece each of bias tape and cording. Unfold tape and press flat. Fold tape over cording and machine-baste, using zipper foot and sewing close to cording. Pin flap front, right side up, to batting. With raw edges aligned, baste cording to flap front from dot to dot (along sides and top), using ⅝″ seam allowance. Clip tape at curves. Sew flap front to flap back (right sides together), using ⅝″ seam allowance and leaving bottom edges open. Trim batting seam to ¼″. Turn flap and press; machine-baste bottom edges.

Pockets

1. Cut two large pocket pieces from pindot and one from interfacing; transfer pleat markings to right side of one pindot piece. For small pocket, trim pattern as marked and cut one from pindot; transfer markings to right side. For top-edge binding, cut a 2½" x 15¾" strip from pindot and a 1" x 14" strip from batting. Cut a 1¼" x 11½" pindot strip for bottom-edge binding.

2. Trace mouse, two ears, and two inner ears onto paper side of web. Cut a piece of corduroy large enough to back mouse and ears; cut a piece of velour to back inner ears. Following manufacturer's instructions, fuse web pieces to wrong side of fabric pieces. Trim fabric pieces to match web pieces; remove paper backing. Position mouse on small pocket, tucking one end of the ⅛" ribbon under mouse; fuse mouse. Position and fuse ear pieces.

Cut a piece of lightweight paper large enough to back mouse; pin to wrong side of small pocket. Set machine for appliqué. Using matching thread and satin stitch, appliqué pieces; tear away paper. Embroider mouse as indicated on patterns.

3. Position interfacing between large pocket pieces (wrong sides together) and machine-baste edges. Turn top edge of small pocket under ¼" and press; turn under ¼" again and stitch. With side and bottom edges aligned, pin small pocket (right side up) to large pocket; baste aligned edges. Fold pockets on center line with right sides together. Stitch along pleat line; backstitch to secure. Open seam with pencil and press flat; baste across bottom of pleat. Stitch small pocket as marked; backstitch.

4. Fold eyelet in half and mark center. Align straight edge of eyelet with top edge of pocket and match centers; baste.

Fold fabric strip for top binding with wrong sides and long edges together; press and open. Hand-baste batting strip to wrong side of fabric strip, ¼" from one long edge. With right sides together and centers matched, pin binding strip (side with batting) to top edge of pocket; stitch along back of pocket, following basting stitches. Flip binding up; press raw edge under ¼" and whipstitch to back of pocket. Remove basting stitches.

Position pockets on mattress flap. Turn side edges of pockets (including eyelet) under ¼" and whipstitch to back of flap, sewing securely.

5. Stitch center line, from bottom edge of top binding to top of pleat, sewing through all layers (excluding eyelet); backstitch. Mark center of flat lace and pin ¼" from bottom edge of pocket; baste. Mark center of strip for bottom-edge binding and match to center of bottom edge (right sides together); sew, using lace-basting stitches on pocket as a guide. Turn under ends of binding ¼" and press. Wrap ends toward back of flap; turn under again and whipstitch securely. Turn bottom edge of binding under ¼". Fold to back of flap and slipstitch edge.

6. Loop mouse tail and tack loops in place. Tie blue ribbon into a bow and tack near end of tail; trim ends of bow.

Kitty Cat

1. Cut pieces for body, head, and outer ears as marked. Trace inner ear (twice) and nose onto paper side of web. Fuse web pieces to ribbon scraps, using yellow for inner ears and peach for nose. Trim ribbon scraps to match web pieces. Cut a 1½" x 10½" strip from velour for tail. From print fabric, cut two 5½" squares for bow and a 1½" x 2½" piece for bow band.

2. For body, stack from bottom, in this order: batting, front (right side up), back (right side down); sew, leaving opening as marked. Clip curves; turn body and press lightly. Whipstitch opening closed.

3. Remove paper from web pieces. Using tip of iron, fuse inner ears to two outer ears; fuse nose to front of head (either piece). Appliqué pieces, same as mouse. Embroider remaining facial features as indicated on pattern.

4. With right sides together, sew two ear pieces as marked. Repeat for remaining ear. Turn ears and press lightly. With raw edges aligned, baste ears (right side down) to front of head as marked.

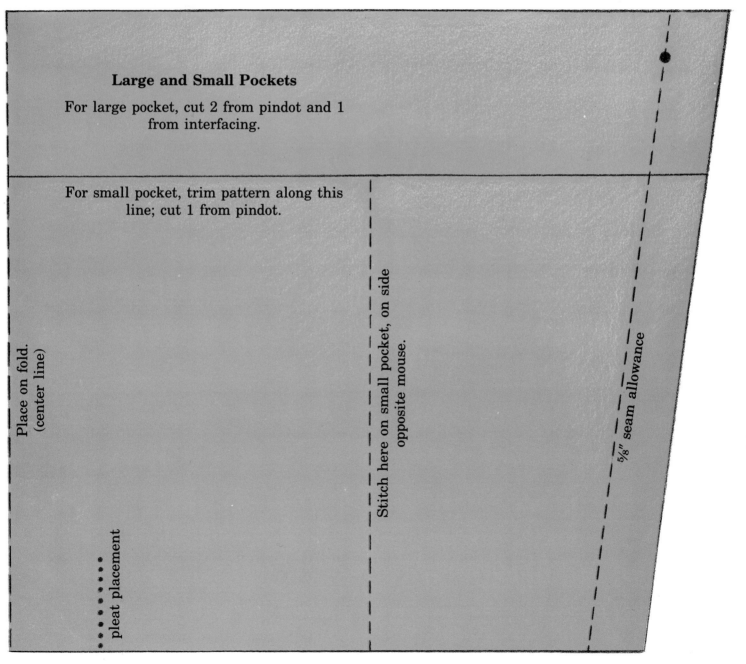

Large and Small Pockets

For large pocket, cut 2 from pindot and 1 from interfacing.

For small pocket, trim pattern along this line; cut 1 from pindot.

Place on fold. (center line)

pleat placement

Stitch here on small pocket, on side opposite mouse.

5/8" seam allowance

5. For head, stack two batting pieces, back of head (right side up), and front of head (right side down); pin and sew, leaving opening as marked. Turn head and press lightly; whipstitch opening closed.

Position body and head on flap so that bottom of body and face are approximately ½″ inside pocket. Whipstitch pieces to each other and to flap.

6. With right sides together, sew fabric squares for bow, leaving opening for turning. Clip corners; turn and press bow. Whipstitch opening closed. Gather center of bow with a running stitch. Fold bow band in thirds, lengthwise, enclosing one raw edge. Wrap band around bow; turn ends of band under and whipstitch together. Tack bow to body.

7. Sew tail pieces with right sides together, leaving one end open. Clip corners; turn tail and press lightly. Zigzag-stitch open end. With tail pointing up and edges aligned, whipstitch zigzagged edge to bottom edge of body as marked; machine-stitch across tail, 1″ from zigzagged edge, sewing through tail, body, and flap. With tail pointing down, turn end up 1½″ and tack securely.

Key to Embroidery Stitches

(Use three strands in color indicated.)
s st—satin stitch
b st—backstitch
Fr knt—French knot
out—outline stitch

110

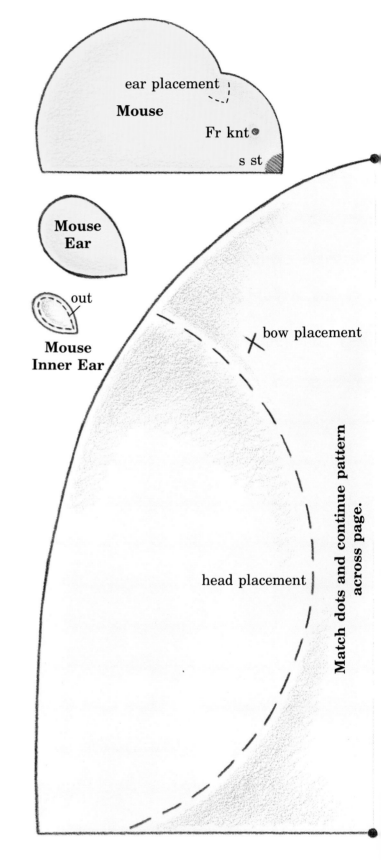

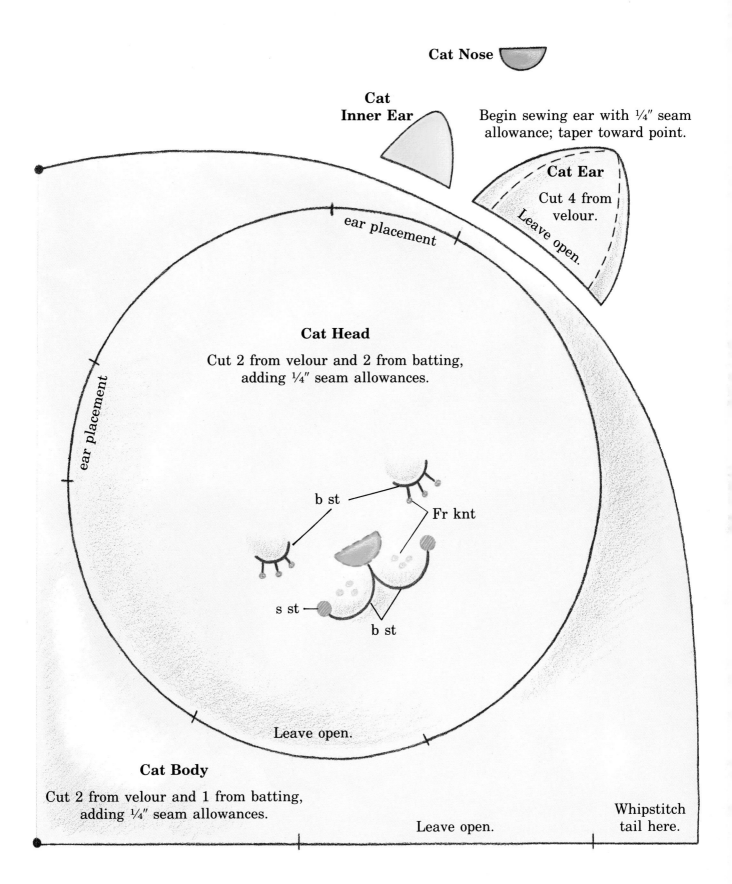

Cat Nose

Cat Inner Ear

Begin sewing ear with ¼″ seam allowance; taper toward point.

Cat Ear

Cut 4 from velour.

Leave open.

ear placement

ear placement

Cat Head

Cut 2 from velour and 2 from batting, adding ¼″ seam allowances.

b st

Fr knt

s st

b st

Leave open.

Cat Body

Cut 2 from velour and 1 from batting, adding ¼″ seam allowances.

Leave open.

Whipstitch tail here.

Cross-Stitched Cowboy

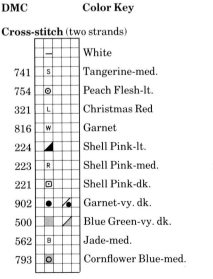

What is the stuff of a little boy's dreams? Cowboy boots and a ten-gallon hat, a pony all his own, and a midnight ride under star-studded skies.

Stitched on white Aida 14 over one thread, the finished design size (pictured here) is 5″ x 7″. The fabric was cut 13″ x 15″.

You will need:
Cross-stitch fabric
Blunt tapestry needle
Embroidery floss

1. Cut fabric at least 3″ larger on all sides than finished design size. Whipstitch or machine-zigzag raw edges.

2. Fold fabric from top to bottom and from left to right to locate center. Begin stitching at center, following the graph and color key.

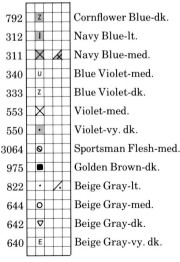
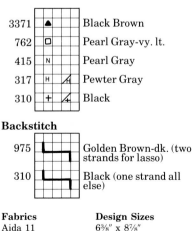

DMC   Color Key

Cross-stitch (two strands)

DMC	Symbol	Color
	–	White
741	S	Tangerine-med.
754	⊙	Peach Flesh-lt.
321	L	Christmas Red
816	W	Garnet
224	◣	Shell Pink-lt.
223	R	Shell Pink-med.
221	⊡	Shell Pink-dk.
902	● /	Garnet-vy. dk.
500	/	Blue Green-vy. dk.
562	B	Jade-med.
793	⊙	Cornflower Blue-med.

DMC	Symbol	Color
792	Z	Cornflower Blue-dk.
312	I	Navy Blue-lt.
311	X /	Navy Blue-med.
340	U	Blue Violet-med.
333	Z	Blue Violet-dk.
553	X	Violet-med.
550	·	Violet-vy. dk.
3064	⊘	Sportsman Flesh-med.
975	■	Golden Brown-dk.
822	· /	Beige Gray-lt.
644	O	Beige Gray-med.
642	▽	Beige Gray-dk.
640	E	Beige Gray-vy. dk.

DMC	Symbol	Color
3371	▲	Black Brown
762	▢	Pearl Gray-vy. lt.
415	N	Pearl Gray
317	H /	Pewter Gray
310	+ /	Black

Backstitch

DMC	Symbol	Color
975	⌐	Golden Brown-dk. (two strands for lasso)
310	⌐	Black (one strand all else)

Fabrics	Design Sizes
Aida 11	6⅜″ x 8⅞″
Aida 18	3⅞″ x 5½″
Hardanger 22	3⅛″ x 4½″

Stitch Count

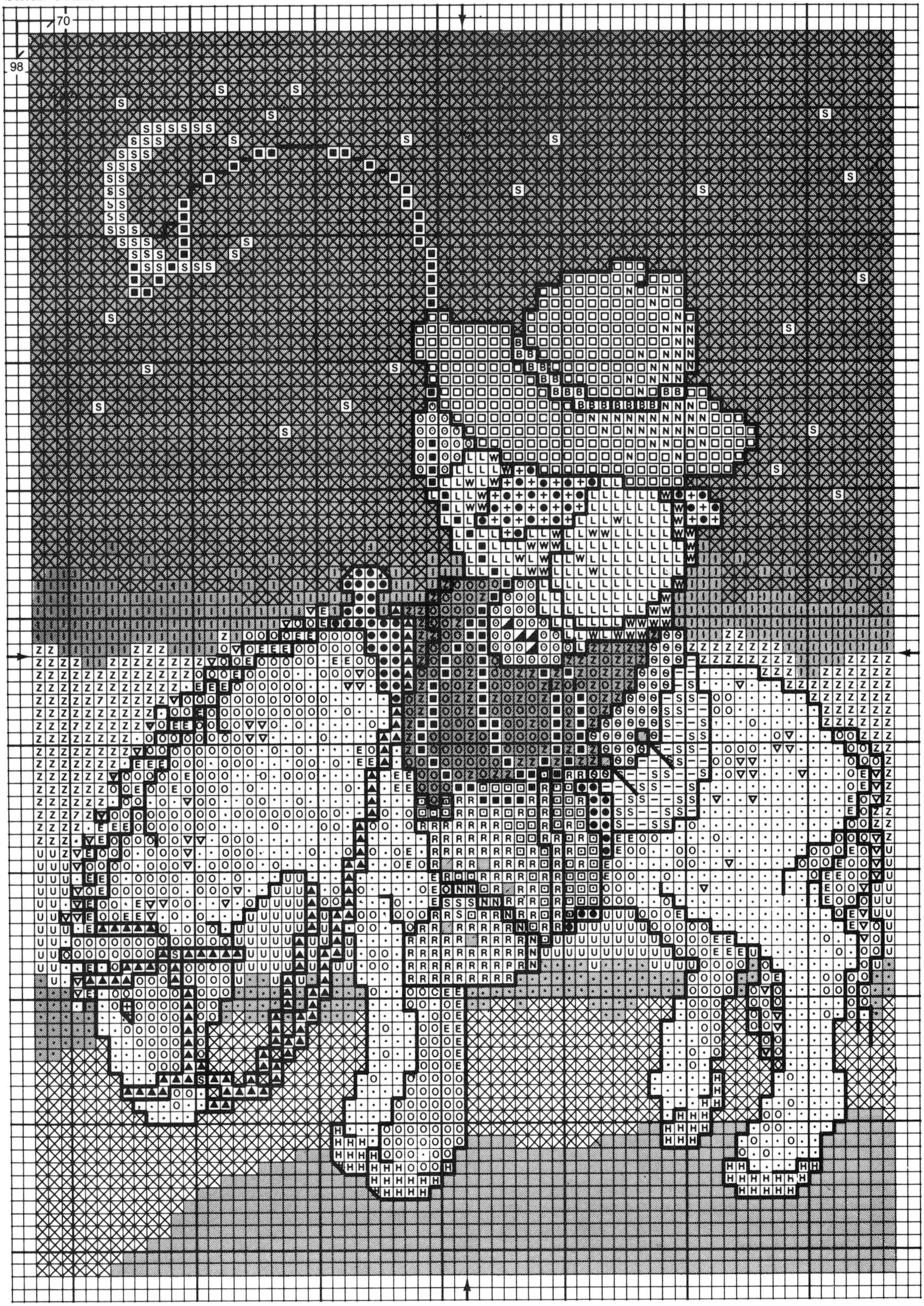

Paperdoll Screen

Whether acting as a playful or a practical piece, this screen promises to be a bedroom star. The panels are simple plywood shapes, joined with hinges and then painted to resemble three life-size dolls. Patterns are provided, but if you're especially talented, consider drawing and painting the dolls in the likeness of the lucky one who'll find this gift under the tree.

You will need:
Metal tape measure
1½' x 4' piece of butcher paper
4' x 8' (⅜") best-grade plywood
  Electric saber saw
   4 (6-foot) 1 x 1s plus 1 (4-foot) 1 x 1
   Electric drill with ⅛" bit
   30 (1⅛") #8 oval wood screws
   Wood glue
   4 small hinges (1½" square is good
      size) and wood screws
   Wood filler
   Sandpaper
   Paintbrushes
   Latex primer
   Carbon paper
   Acrylic paint

1. Enlarge pattern for panel to full size on butcher paper; cut out. Draw around pattern three times on back of plywood, with top of pattern positioned at one 8′ edge; cut out panels with the saw.

2. To make a support frame for each panel, cut two 32″ pieces from a 1 x 1. Using the ⅛″ bit, drill holes through each piece, 2″ from either end and one through the center. Glue pieces to back of panel, at sides, and secure with screws. Measure width of panel between ends of 1 x 1s; cut pieces from remaining pieces of 1 x 1 to fit. Drill a hole 2″ from end of each piece. Glue pieces to panel and secure with screws. (Figure A.)

Figure A

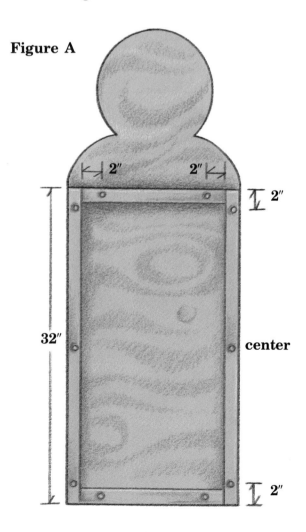

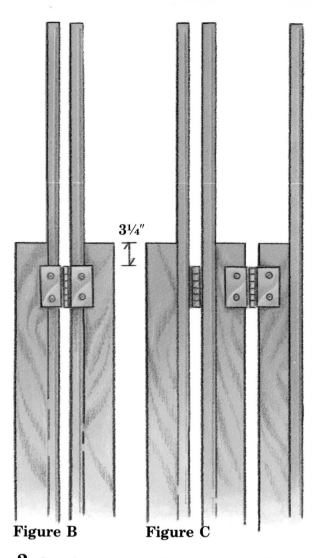

Figure B   **Figure C**

3. Stand two panels front to front. Mount a hinge, with knuckles out, on edges, 3¼″ from top of frame (Figure B); mount another hinge 8″ from bottom of frame. Stand remaining panel back to back with center panel. On unhinged side of panels, mount a hinge on edges, 3¼″ from top (Figure C) and 8″ from bottom.

4. Use wood filler as needed; let dry. Sand panels smooth. Apply primer; let dry and sand lightly again.

5. Enlarge doll to full size on panel pattern, using grid and full-size patterns. Cut out doll. On each panel, draw around the doll; transfer features, using carbon paper. Add details. Using dark paint, outline the dolls (all features). Paint as desired, applying several coats of paint and letting the paint dry between coats.

116

Patterns for Panel and Doll
One square = 2".

Patterns for Arms and Shoes

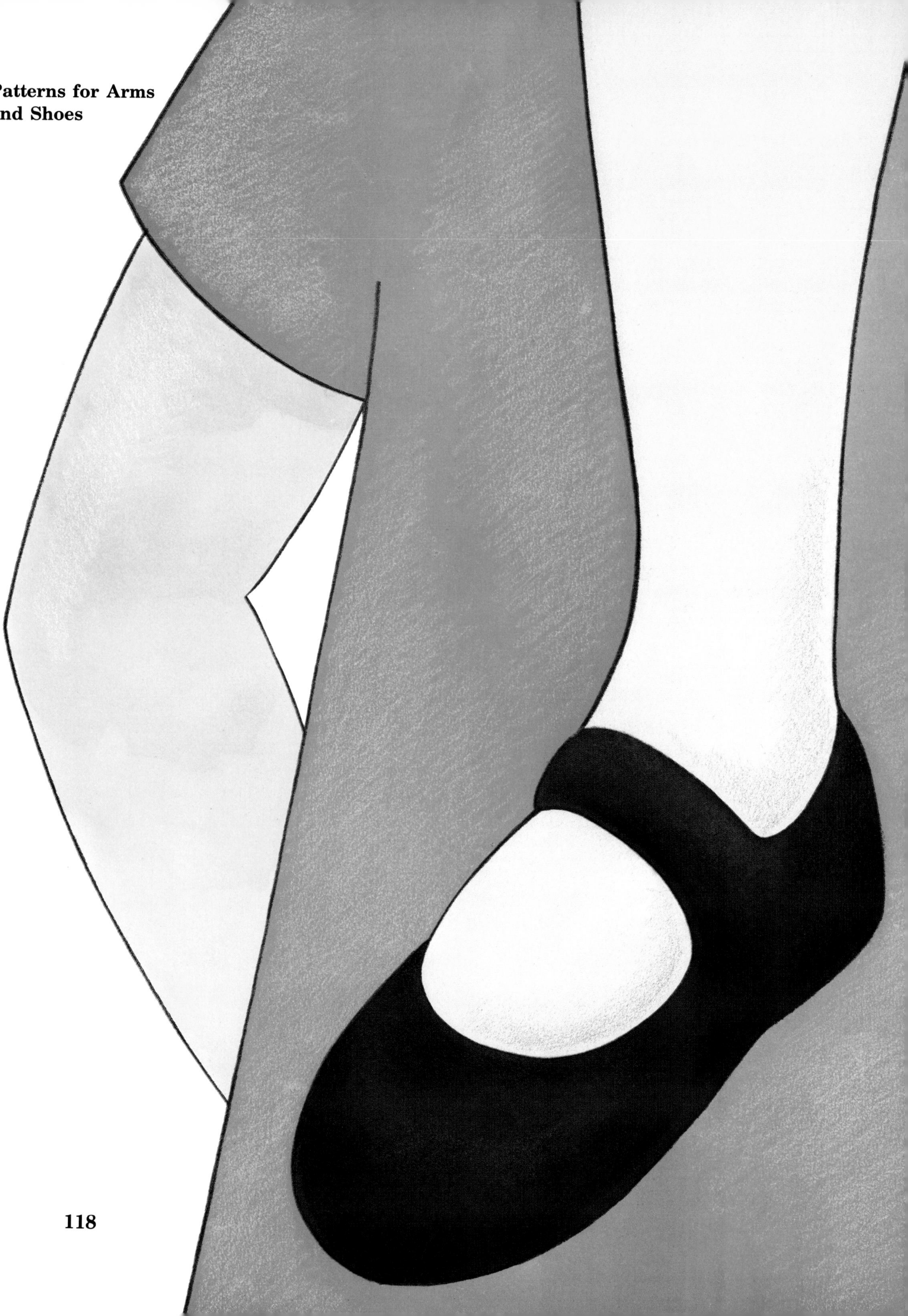

Pattern for Face

Push Chick

A toddler's idea of a terrific new toy? Brightly colored with non-stop get-up-and-go!

You will need:
4″ x 8″ (⅞″-thick) pine
4″ x 24″ (½″-thick) pine
Scroll saw (or jigsaw)
Electric drill with ⅜″, ¼″, and ⅛″ bits
Sandpaper
5¼″ (¼″-diameter) wooden dowel for axle
23″ (⅜″-diameter) wooden dowel for push stick
1″ wooden bead with ⅜″ hole
Paintbrushes
Acrylic paint (yellow, orange, and black)
Clear acrylic spray enamel
4″ x 12″ piece of orange vinyl
White glue
C-clamp and protective pads
2 metal washers with ⅜″ holes
Tapestry needle
Orange embroidery floss
28″ (⅝″-wide) ribbon

1. Transfer patterns for chick, wings, and wheels to back of pine pieces as marked. Cut out the pieces, using the scroll saw; cut slit in each wheel.

2. Measure and mark centers of side edges of chick, 1″ up from bottom edge. Using the drill and ⅜″ bit, drill a hole through center of one edge, all the way through center of other edge. On back of chick, locate center, 3″ up from bottom edge; drill a ⅜″ hole (for push stick) at a downward slant. Drill a ⅜″ hole through each wing, a ¼″ hole through each wheel, and a ⅛″ hole through top of chick's head, as marked on patterns.

3. Sand chick and dowels smooth. Paint chick, wings, ⅜″ dowel, and bead yellow; paint the wheels orange. Let pieces dry and sand lightly. Apply several more coats of paint, letting the paint dry between coats and after the final coat. Paint features and let dry. Spray pieces with clear acrylic enamel. Let dry.

4. Transfer pattern for feet to vinyl and cut as marked. Glue two pieces for each foot, wrong sides together, and let dry. Use a piece of sandpaper to separate slits in wheels, if necessary. Glue feet inside slits as marked. Let dry.

5. Glue wings to body, right sides out, aligning holes. Clamp together and let dry.

6. Wax the ¼″ dowel with paraffin or soap and slide through chick and wings. Slip washers on dowel. Glue wheels onto dowel, positioning wheels so that feet are flat on floor in front. Paint ends of dowel orange. Let dry.

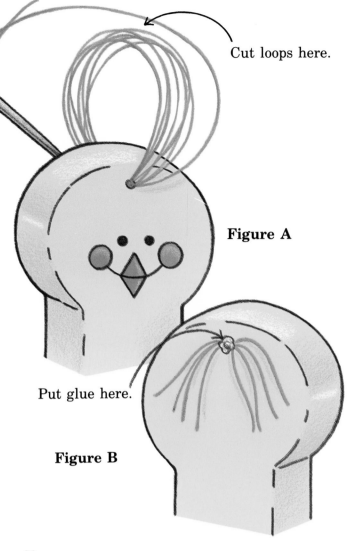

Cut loops here.

Figure A

Put glue here.

Figure B

7. Put glue on one end of the ⅜″ dowel; tap dowel into hole on back of chick. Glue bead at end of dowel and let dry.

8. Thread tapestry needle with floss. On back of chick's head, insert needle through hole, leaving a 2″ tail of floss. Bring needle out front and insert in back again, leaving a 4″ loop. Make eight loops. Cut loops at top. (Figure A.) On back of chick, divide strands in half; put a bead of glue in center. (Figure B.) Tie strands together; trim ends to 1″. Repeat with strands on front of chick.

9. Tie ribbon in a bow around chick's neck.

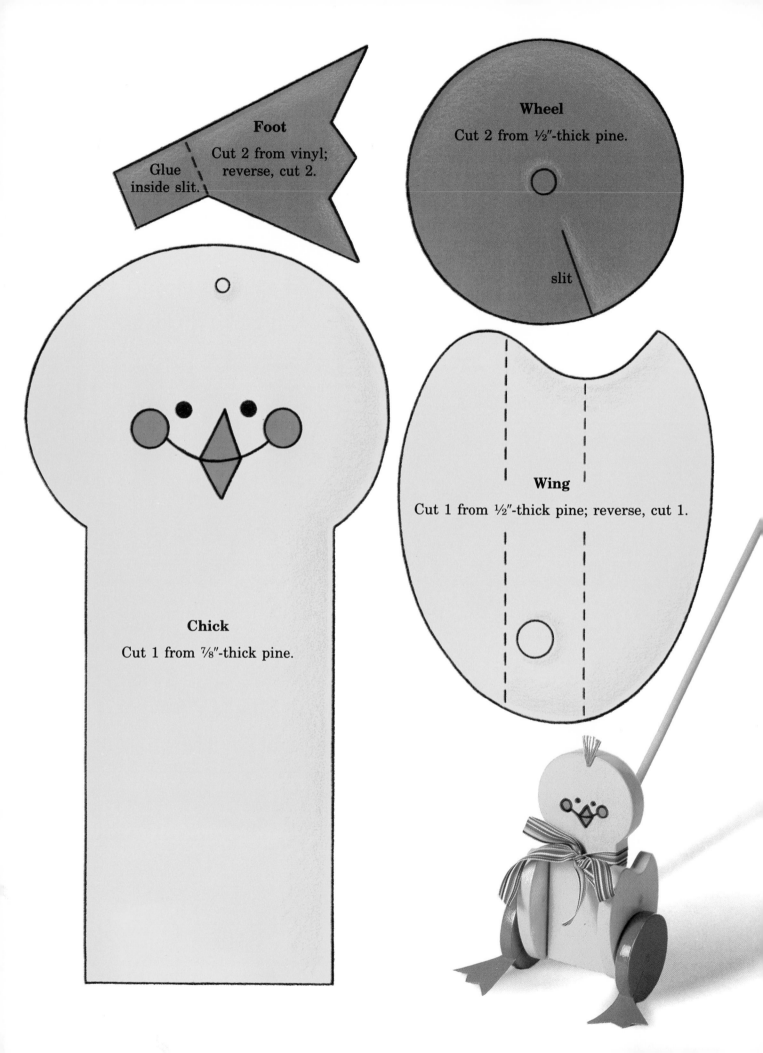

Foot
Cut 2 from vinyl;
reverse, cut 2.

Glue
inside slit.

Wheel
Cut 2 from ½″-thick pine.

slit

Wing
Cut 1 from ½″-thick pine; reverse, cut 1.

Chick
Cut 1 from ⅞″-thick pine.

Holiday Fun Folder

Tops on the list of great gifts for kids is this cute keeper. The cover features a stocking (just the right size for pencils), "stuffed" with the most famous reindeer of all. Inside are pockets for stickers, paints, crayons, and other supplies.

You will need:
Scraps of Christmas-print fabrics for stocking and antlers
Scraps of brown fabric for reindeer
⅓ yard (36″-wide) quilted fabric for folder and pockets
12″ x 20½″ piece of Christmas-print fabric for lining

Thread to match fabrics
6″ square of lightweight fusible interfacing
12″ square of fusible web
24″ pindot bias tape
1 yard (⅝″-wide) ribbon
2 (8½″ x 10″) pieces of cardboard
2 (½″) wiggly eyes
1 (½″) pom-pom
Black fine-tip marker
6″ (⅜″-wide) ribbon for stocking bow
7 small snowflake-shaped beads
2 small brass bells

Note: Use ¼″ seam allowances throughout project.

1. Transfer appliqué patterns and cut as marked. From quilted fabric, cut one 12″ x 20½″ piece (for folder) and two 6″ x 12″ pieces (for pockets). Fold folder piece with wrong sides and 12″ edges together; press and open. On wrong side of folder piece, mark top and bottom of center fold.

2. Fuse interfacing stocking to wrong side of fabric stocking. Cut a 1″ x 3″ strip from fabric used for stocking patches. With right sides together, sew one 3″ edge of strip to top edge of stocking. Flip strip right side up and press. Fold strip to wrong side of stocking and press again, to form binding.

With fabric pieces (right side up) on web pieces, position toe and heel patches on stocking; fuse the pieces, following instructions of web manufacturer. Set machine for appliqué. Using satin stitch, appliqué the patches, stitching only the patch edges that are within the stocking.

3. On right side of folder piece, position and pin stocking, referring to photograph for placement. Using satin stitch, appliqué the stocking, leaving the top edge open; satin-stitch edges again. Position and fuse antlers, head, and hooves. Starting with antlers, appliqué each piece twice, using satin stitch.

4. Cut bias tape in half and sew a piece to one 12″ edge of each pocket piece, finishing edges. Cut the ⅝″-wide ribbon in half. With folder piece right side up, position a ribbon end at center of each 12″ edge, with remaining ribbon ends toward center of folder piece. With right sides together, pin 12″ raw edges of pocket pieces to 12″ edges of folder piece; stitch (with ribbon end between), being careful not to catch free ends of ribbons in stitching. Press seams open.

124

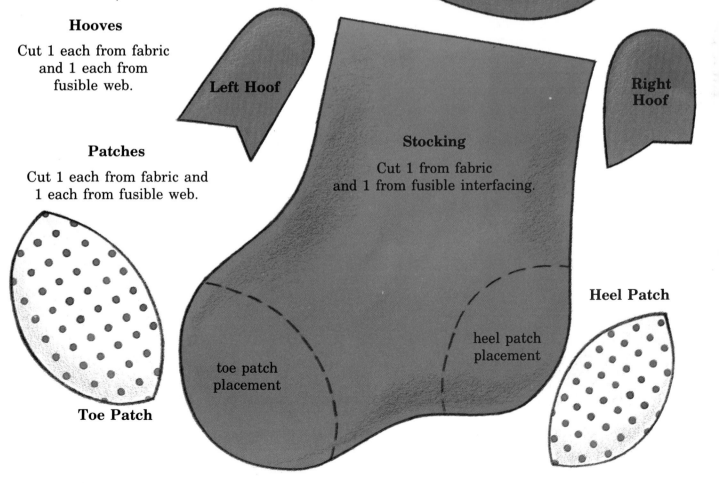

Antlers

Cut 1 from fabric and 1 from fusible web.

5. Fold piece of fabric for lining with wrong sides and 12″ edges together; press. Open lining; on wrong side, mark top and bottom of center fold. Turn 12″ edges under ¼″ toward wrong side of lining; press and stitch. With wrong sides together and center marks aligned, sew lining to folder, stitching ¼″ from top and bottom edges. (Do not stitch 12″ side edges.) Turn folder right side out and press. Stitch lining along center fold from top to bottom edge, backstitching at edges. Insert a cardboard piece through each open end of lining. Fold pockets toward lining, tucking raw edges under ¼″; whipstitch top and bottom edges to folder.

6. Glue eyes and nose to reindeer face. Using the fine-tip marker, draw mouth and eyebrows. Tie the 6″ piece of ribbon into a bow and tack to stocking; sew beads to folder. Tie a bell onto end of each ⅝″ ribbon; tie ribbons into a bow.

eye placement

nose placement

Head

Cut 1 from fabric and 1 from fusible web.

Hooves

Cut 1 each from fabric and 1 each from fusible web.

Left Hoof

Right Hoof

Patches

Cut 1 each from fabric and 1 each from fusible web.

Stocking

Cut 1 from fabric and 1 from fusible interfacing.

Heel Patch

heel patch placement

toe patch placement

Toe Patch

Honeybear Purse

Ahh . . . looks like a case of love at first sight.

You will need:

9″ x 12″ piece of white felt
6″ square of brown fabric
⅛ yard (36″-wide) pink fabric
2 (4″ x 6″) pieces of black fabric
2 (6″) squares each of green and lavender
   fabric
½ yard (45″-wide) pink-and-white dotted
   swiss
Thread to match
Scrap of red felt
½ yard (18″-wide) fusible web
¼ yard (24″-wide) fleece
4″ embroidery hoop
Embroidery needle and floss (white, black,
   yellow)
1½ yards (⅞″-wide) grosgrain ribbon

Making the Appliqués

1. Using the eye pattern, cut two circles each from white felt and web. Transfer eye pattern twice to brown fabric. Place brown fabric in hoop. Using three strands of floss and satin stitch, embroider whites and pupils of eyes. Cut out eyes, adding ¼″ seam allowance. On wrong side of eyes, center web and then felt circles; fuse, following manufacturer's instructions. Clip curves and press seam allowance to wrong side.

2. Cut inner ears and cheeks as marked on patterns. On wrong side of pink pieces, center web and then felt pieces; fuse. Clip curves and press ¼″ seam allowances to wrong side.

3. Cut a 4″ x 6″ piece of web and fuse the two black fabric pieces, wrong sides together. Transfer nose/mouth pattern to fabric. Appliqué all lines, using narrow satin stitch; stitch again. Cut out piece, cutting close to, but not into, stitching.

4. Cut a 6″ square of web and fuse the green fabric squares, wrong sides to-gether. Transfer leaf pattern to fabric square. Appliqué all lines and cut out piece, using same procedure as for nose/mouth.

5. Transfer pattern for flower and bee to right side of one lavender fabric square. Place fabric in hoop. Using three strands of floss and satin stitch, embroider bee's body yellow and head black. Using three strands of black, outline body with back-stitch and straight-stitch antennae. Em-broider wings with one strand of white floss and straight stitch.

Cut a 6″ square of web and fuse laven-der squares, wrong sides together. Appli-qué outline of flower and cut out piece, using same procedure as for nose/mouth. Sew center bead to flower as marked, stitching through all layers; sew remain-ing beads around center bead.

6. Transfer patterns for mouth and tongue, and cut as marked. Sew mouth pieces, right sides together, along marked seamline. Clip curves. Turn mouth right side out and fold as marked; press. Posi-tion straight edge of tongue inside fold and sew as shown. (Figure A.)

Figure A

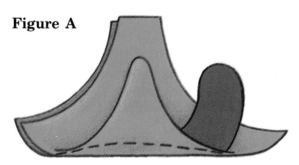

Stitch from edge to edge, widening seam to ⅛″ at center and catching straight edge of tongue in seam.

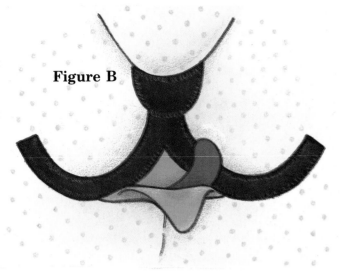

Figure B

Making the Purse

1. Transfer patterns for purse and cut as marked. Pin fleece pieces to wrong sides of one set of dotted swiss pieces (forehead, two ears, two lower faces, back of head). These will be referred to as lined pieces.

2. Pin pair of lined lower-face pieces, right sides together, at center front; stitch from dot to bottom edge. Stitch lined lower face to lined forehead, making one complete lined face. Repeat with unlined pieces to make unlined face. Grade seams on lined face. On both faces, clip curves and press seams open.

3. Pin nose/mouth to right side of unlined face, with top of nose at curve of forehead/lower face seam. Position raw edges of pink mouth ¼″ under center of nose/mouth, forcing lower pink mouth downward (Figure B); pin. Pin cheek appliqués, overlapping ends of black mouth. Center eyes on face seam, 1″ up from ends of nose, and pin. With matching thread, hand-appliqué pieces to face.

4. Center inner ear appliqués on right sides of two unlined ears and pin. Hand-appliqué, using pink thread. With right sides together, pin appliquéd ears to lined ears. Stitch curved edges, leaving straight edges open. Trim fleece seam allowance to ⅛″; trim dotted swiss seam allowance to ¼″. Clip curves and turn ears.

5. With appliquéd sides together and raw edges aligned, pin ears to unlined face, centering ears on forehead/lower face seams. With right sides together and raw edges aligned, pin lined face to unlined face; stitch all around, leaving an opening at center bottom for turning. Trim seam allowances as in step 4. Clip curves. Turn face and slipstitch opening closed.

6. Layer dotted swiss back-of-head pieces, with right sides together and fleece on top. Stitch all around, leaving an opening at center bottom for turning. Trim seam allowances as in step 4 and clip curves. Turn; slipstitch opening closed.

7. For shoulder strap, measure length of ribbon to fit child and add 4″. Turn ribbon ends up 1″ and fold in half lengthwise; pin to back of head as marked, being careful not to twist ribbon. Bar-tack ribbon to purse. (Figure C.)

8. Pin wrong side of face to back of head. Starting ½″ above one forehead/lower-face seam, topstitch down side, across bottom, and up other side of purse, stitching close to edge and stopping ½″ above opposite seam. (Leave top of purse open.)

9. Tie remaining piece of ribbon into a bow and tack to face at center front seam; trim ends of bow. Tack flower to leaf; tack leaf and flower to purse, referring to photograph for placement.

Figure C

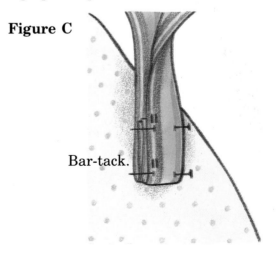

Bar-tack.

Appliqué Patterns

Leaf

¼″ seam allowance

Inner Ear
Cut 2 from pink.
Trim away seam
allowance on pattern;
cut 2 each from
white felt and
fusible web.

½″ seam allowance

Flower

center bead

Eye

Cheek
Cut 2 from pink.
Trim away seam
allowance on pattern;
cut 2 each from white
felt and fusible web.

¼″ seam allowance

Nose/Mouth

Tongue
Cut 1 from red felt.

Mouth
Cut 2 from pink.
Fold up along this line.

¼″ seam
allowance

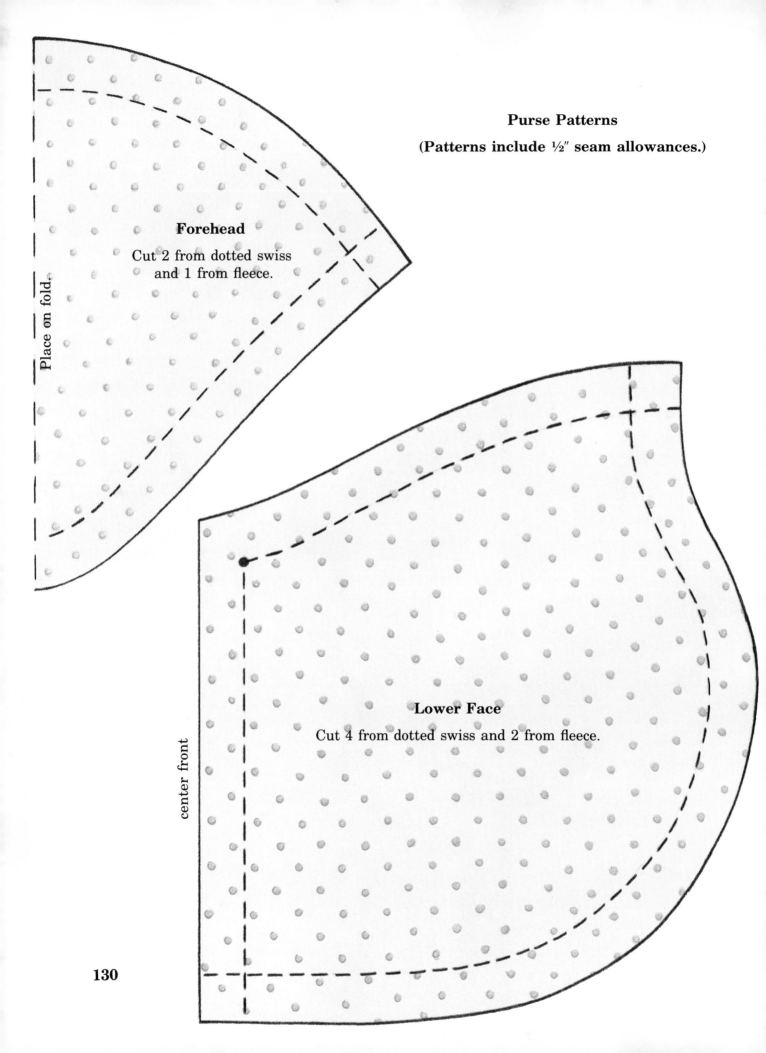

Forehead

Cut 2 from dotted swiss
and 1 from fleece.

Place on fold.

Purse Patterns

(Patterns include ½″ seam allowances.)

Lower Face

Cut 4 from dotted swiss and 2 from fleece.

center front

130

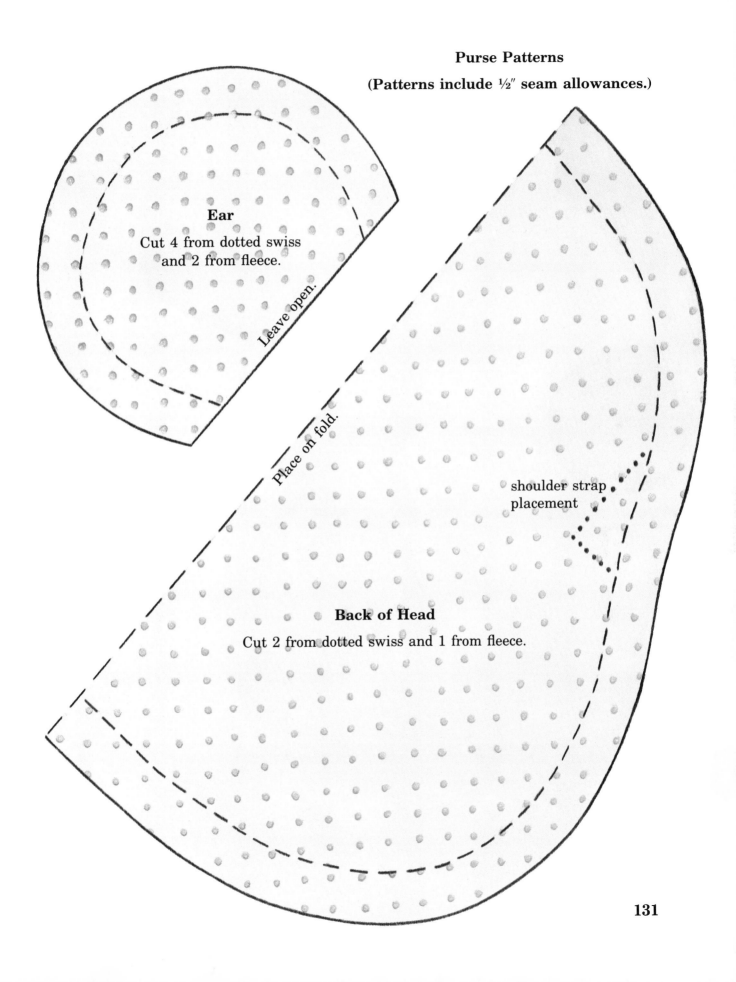

Purse Patterns

(Patterns include ½″ seam allowances.)

Ear

Cut 4 from dotted swiss
and 2 from fleece.

Leave open.

Place on fold.

shoulder strap
placement

Back of Head

Cut 2 from dotted swiss and 1 from fleece.

Oatmeal Babies Necklace

Sweet as pie, these pocket-sized dollies will be the apple of a little girl's eye!

You will need:
Tracing paper
4 (5" x 6") pieces of muslin
Fabric scraps for clothes
2 (3½") squares of fabric for heart
Thread to match fabrics
Polyester stuffing
Razor-point permanent pen
Cotton swab and powdered blush
Embroidery needle and light brown floss
Hot glue gun
1¼ yards (¼"-wide) grosgrain ribbon

Note: Use ⅛" seam allowances throughout the project. When sewing by machine, use a short stitch. To hem clothes, turn edges under ⅛" and hand-stitch, using contrasting thread and a short running stitch (except for waist on pants).

1. Trace and cut out all patterns. Cut pieces for clothes from fabric scraps as marked.

2. To make each baby, draw around pattern on wrong side of one muslin piece. Place marked muslin piece (wrong side up) on a remaining muslin piece (right side up); pin. Machine-stitch outline of baby, leaving opening as marked. Trim, leaving ⅛" seam allowance. Clip curves. Turn baby right side out and press; stuff firmly, keeping shape flat. Slip-stitch opening closed.

3. Using the razor-point pen, draw eyes and mouth on faces. Apply blush to cheeks with cotton swab. To make hair, thread embroidery needle with five strands of floss. Starting at back of baby's head, bring needle to front and make five loops, as marked on pattern.

4. To make pants, place two pant pieces with right sides together and machine-stitch inner and outer leg seams; hem pant legs. Using a long running stitch, hem waist, but do not tie off. Turn pants right side out and place on baby. Pull thread to gather waist; knot thread.

5. Starting at neck edge, cut a 1″ slit down center back of one dress piece. With right sides together, sew dress piece with slit (dress back) to a remaining dress piece (dress front), at shoulders. Press seams open. Place dress front and dress facing with right sides together, matching neck openings; pin. Machine-stitch facing as marked, pivoting needle at point of V. Clip curves; turn facing to inside and press lightly. Hem sleeves and bottom edges of dress pieces. With right sides together, machine-stitch underarm and side seams. Clip seams; turn and press dress. Repeat for second dress. Place dresses on babies and tack neck openings.

6. To make each bonnet, place two bonnet pieces with right sides together, and machine-stitch curved edges (back of bonnet). Press seam open. Hem bonnet edges all around. Put small amount of glue on back of each baby's head. Turn bonnets right side out and place on babies' heads.

7. Trace heart pattern onto wrong side of one fabric square. Place marked square (wrong side up) on remaining fabric square (right side up); pin. Machine-stitch around heart, leaving opening as marked. Trim heart, leaving ⅛″ seam allowance. Clip curves. Turn and press heart; stuff firmly, keeping shape flat. Slip-stitch opening closed.

8. Using thread to match hands, tack heart to babies, at hands. Cut ribbon into two 14½″ pieces. Turn one end of each ribbon under ¼″ and tack to free hand. Cut remaining ribbon in half and tie each piece into a bow. Glue bow to front of each dress.

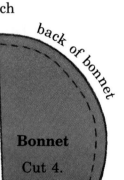

back of bonnet

Bonnet

Cut 4.

Pants

Cut 4.

outer leg

inner leg

Place on fold.

Dress

Cut 4.

Place on fold.

center back

Oatmeal Baby

Cut 4.

Leave open.

Dress Facing

Cut 2.

Heart

Cut 2.

Leave open.

134

TuTu and Tango

Meet TuTu Tallulah and Tango the Tiger, a dynamic duo—born to dance!

You will need (for each doll):

Fabrics (45″-wide)

For **TuTu:** 1⅛ yard pink polka-dot, ⅓ yard teal, ⅓ yard yellow, ⅛ yard red, ⅛ yard teal dot, 1½ yards teal print, 1½ yards pink net

For **Tango:** ⅔ yard yellow, ⅔ yard orange stripe, 1 yard orange, ⅛ yard red, ⅛ yard yellow stripe

Thread to match

Water-soluble marking pen

Drawing compass

½ yard paper-backed fusible web

30″ (¼″-wide) elastic

4 to 5 (12-ounce) bags polyester stuffing

Sharp hand-sewing, 4″ soft-sculpture, and tapestry needles

2 (½″) black shank buttons (for eyes)

Heavy-duty black thread

Red and black embroidery floss

For **TuTu:** 1 yard batting, 4″ x 7″ piece of cardboard, 1 skein medium-weight yellow yarn, small hook and eye, 20 yellow diamond-shaped shank buttons (for shoes), 3½ yards (¼″-wide) yellow ribbon

For **Tango:** 3½″ x 10″ piece of batting, 14 (½″) red round shank buttons (for shoes), 4 (½″) red buttons (for straps), 1⅔ yards (⅜″-wide) orange ribbon, 20″ (¼″-wide) elastic, 1 pair (⅜″-wide and 37″-long) yellow shoestrings

Cutting Out the Dolls

1. For **TuTu,** trace patterns for paws, shoes, and head, and cut as marked. From pink dot, cut two 10″ x 12½″ pieces (body), two 6″ x 9″ pieces (arms), two 6″ x 10″ pieces (legs), and one 1¼″ x 12″ strip (paw straps). From teal, cut two 3″ x 10″ pieces (shoe tops), two 6⅛″-diameter circles (shoe bottoms), and one 1¼″ x 16″ strip (shoe straps).

For ears, cut traced head pattern apart, 5⅝″ from bottom edge. Spread pattern pieces 7¾″ apart on a piece of paper; draw ear. Cut two ears each from pink dot, yellow, and batting.

On paper side of web, trace patterns for nose, two heart cheeks, and eight paw pads. Fuse web pieces to wrong side of fabric pieces, using red for nose and cheeks and yellow for paw pads. Cut out the fused pieces.

2. For **Tango,** transfer patterns for paws, shoes, head, and outer ears, and cut as marked. From orange stripe, cut two 10″ x 12½″ pieces (body), two 6″ x 9″ pieces (arms), two 6″ x 10″ pieces (legs), and one 5″ x 17″ strip (tail). From orange, cut two 6⅛″-diameter circles (shoe bottoms), one 1¼″ x 12″ strip (paw straps), and one 1¼″ x 16″ strip (for shoe straps). From red, cut two 3″ x 10″ pieces (shoe tops).

On paper side of web, trace patterns for eight paw pads, nose, two inner ears, and 16 "stripes" (four for each side of the head, front and back). Fuse web pieces to wrong side of following fabric pieces: yellow for paw pads, red for nose, and orange for inner ears and stripes. Cut out the fused pieces.

Note: Use ¼″ seam allowances throughout project unless instructed otherwise. Add stuffing to dolls in small quantities and pack firmly, with the aid of a crochet needle or wooden spoon handle.

Making TuTu

1. For front of head, sew two pieces, right sides together, at center. Remove paper backing from nose and cheeks; position pieces on head front and fuse. Set machine for appliqué. Using matching thread and satin stitch, appliqué the pieces. For back of head, sew remaining head pieces, with right sides together, at center.

2. For each ear, place pink dot ear and yellow ear, right sides together, on top of batting ear. Stitch, using ½″ seam allowance and leaving bottom open. Trim batting seam to ⅛″; clip points and curves. Turn and press.

Fold each ear lengthwise, with yellow on inside and bottom edges aligned; baste across bottom, near edge. With raw edges aligned, baste ears to right side of head front, on either side of center front seam. (Figure A.) With right sides together, sew head front to head back, keeping ends of ears out of the way and leaving bottom of head open. Turn head right side out.

3. For two paw straps, cut one 14″ piece of ¼″ elastic. Lay the 1¼″ x 14″ fabric

Figure A

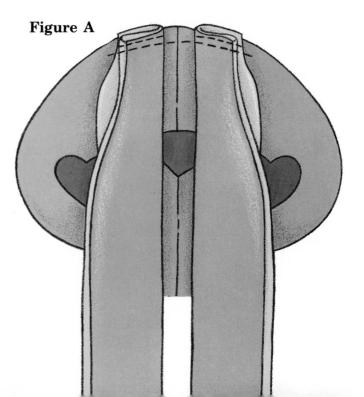

strip (already cut) with wrong side up. Fold one long edge of strip ¼″ toward center and press. Position elastic inside fold and fold edge ¼″ toward center again. Fold and press long raw edge ⅛″ and then ¼″ toward center. Zigzag-stitch strap, stretching elastic as you sew. Cut strap in half. Repeat with a 16″ piece of elastic and the 1¼″ x 16″ fabric strip to make the shoe straps.

4. Remove paper backing from paw pads. Fuse pads to two paw pieces; appliqué pads.

Baste ends of one paw strap to an appliquéd paw piece as marked. With right sides together, sew appliquéd paw to a plain paw, sewing from dot to wrist, in direction indicated by arrow on pattern. Press seam open.

On a 6″ edge of one arm piece, mark a 3″ opening (for stuffing) near center. With right sides together, sew a 9″ edge of same arm piece to wrist of one partially stitched paw, pivoting needle at paw seam. Press seam open. With right sides together and raw edges aligned, finish sewing seam around paw and arm, leaving 3″ and top of arm open. Turn arm right side out. Repeat for second strap, paw, and arm.

5. For each shoe, sew two pieces, right sides together, at front and back, leaving top and bottom open. Baste ends of a shoe strap to each side of the shoe as marked. Pin shoe bottom to shoe, right sides together, and sew. Turn shoe right side out.

With right sides together, pin a 10″ edge of each shoe top to a 10″ edge of a leg piece; sew. Press seam toward shoe top. Mark a 3″ opening near center of one unstitched edge of leg/shoe top. With right sides together, sew unstitched edges together, leaving the opening. Do not turn. Press leg/shoe top flat, with seam at center back.

Tuck a shoe (shoe bottom first) inside leg/shoe top. Pin shoe to shoe top, matching center back seams; stitch. Turn piece right side out.

Figure B

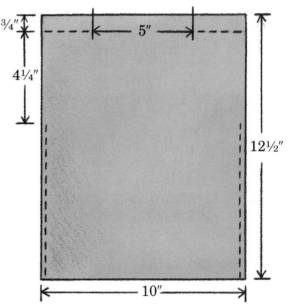

6. Align body pieces, with right sides together, and mark a 5″ neck opening at center. Using ¾″ seam allowance, sew shoulders, backstitching at the 5″ opening. Starting 4¼″ from shoulder seams (to allow openings for arms), sew the side seams. (Figure B.) Do not turn.

With neck up, tuck head (right side out) inside body. With raw edges aligned, pin neck to neck opening, matching side seams of head with shoulder seams. Stitch, using ¾″ seam allowance; stitch again to secure.

Tuck each arm (right side out and paw first) inside body, with thumb facing up. Align raw edges and pin; stitch across arm opening. Turn body and head right side out. With raw edges aligned and toes toward front of body, pin legs to front of body only. Stitch.

7. Firmly stuff arms, head, and body, using approximately one bag of stuffing for head. Slipstitch openings closed with a double strand of matching thread. Firmly stuff legs and slipstitch the openings closed.

8. To make tail, wrap yarn 300 times around the 7″ edges of the cardboard. At each 7″ edge, slip a piece of yarn through the loops and tie; cut the loops down the center of the cardboard at front and back. Tie the two pom-poms together. Using a tapestry needle, sew tail to center back of body, 3½″ up from bottom seam.

9. Using the soft-sculpture needle and four strands of heavy-duty thread, sew on button eyes, sewing through head (back and forth from button to button) and pulling thread slightly to "indent" eyes. Tie off by wrapping thread around one of the buttons and knotting it. To embroider nose/mouth line, use three strands of red floss and outline stitch.

Making Tango

1. Remove paper backing from stripes, nose, and inner ears. On each head piece, position four stripes; fuse. Set machine for appliqué. Using orange thread and satin stitch, appliqué stripes to head pieces. With right sides together and appliquéd edges aligned, sew head front pieces at center; sew head back pieces at center. Using red thread, machine-appliqué nose/mouth lines onto head front.

138

2. For each ear, fuse an inner ear to an outer ear. Appliqué inner ear, using orange thread. Place the appliquéd ear and a plain ear, right sides together, on top of a batting ear; stitch, leaving bottom open. Clip curves; turn and press.

With raw edges aligned, position ears (appliquéd side down) on head front, ¼″ from center front stripes; baste. With right sides together, sew head front to head back, leaving bottom open. Turn head right side out.

3. Follow steps 3 through 6 for TuTu.

4. For tail, fold piece in half lengthwise, with right sides together and stripes aligned; pin. Stitch across one end and down one long edge, leaving a 2″ opening near center of long edge. Turn tail right side out and press flat, with seam at center back. With tail seam up and raw edges aligned, pin tail to center of body front, overlapping the legs; sew.

5. Stuff, same as step 7 for TuTu. Stuff tail and slipstitch closed. Follow step 9 for TuTu, excluding embroidery instructions.

6. To make whiskers, thread soft-sculpture needle with three strands of black floss and tie a knot 3″ from end. Push the needle in at A and out at B. With thread still attached to needle, tie a knot at B, right next to face; trim end to 3″. Repeat, sewing from C to D and from E to F. (Figure C.)

Dressing TuTu

1. Cut three 15″ x 54″ pieces from net (tutu) and one 15″ x 54″ piece from teal print (skirt). From teal dot, cut one 1½″ x 20″ strip (skirt waistband) and two 4″ x 12″ strips (skirt straps). Cut chest heart as marked.

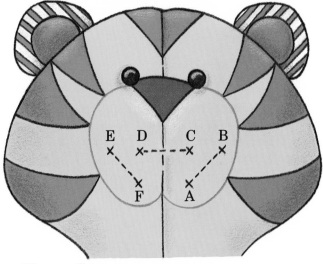

Figure C

2. Stack the three tutu pieces. Machine-baste a row of gathering stitches down lengthwise center, keeping the net smooth and flat; sew gathering stitches down either side of the center line, ¼″ from it.

Fold teal skirt piece with long edges and right sides together. Stitch short edges (side seams). Clip corners; turn and press. Machine-baste a row of gathering stitches, ⅛″ from long raw edges; repeat ¼″ from same edges.

Fold tutu along center gathering line and place skirt (raw edge toward center) inside fold. Mark folded edge into fourths with pins. Gather tutu and skirt to measure 19½″. Fasten off.

3. Mark one long edge of waistband into fourths. Pin right side to gathered edge of tutu/skirt, adjusting gathers to match marked points (waistband will extend ¼″ past either end of skirt); stitch. Turn all raw edges under ¼″ and press. Fold waistband to inside of skirt and slipstitch, covering gathering stitches on skirt. Sew hook and eye to ends of waistband. Place skirt on TuTu.

4. For each strap, fold piece in half with right sides and long edges together. Sew across one end, down long edge (leaving a 1½″ opening near center), and across remaining end. Clip corners. Turn and press; slipstitch opening closed.

With strap ends slightly angled, pin to inside of waistband, 1½″ apart on front and 2″ from waistband ends on back. Slip-stitch straps to waistband.

5. Sew two heart pieces with right sides together, leaving opening as marked. Clip curves and trim point; turn and stuff. Slipstitch opening closed. Tack heart to front straps, 2″ below neck seam.

6. Starting just below leg/shoe top seam, sew five buttons to one shoe, placing the buttons ½″ from center front seam and 1¾″ apart. Repeat on other side of center front shoe seam. (Figure D.) Cut a 45″ piece of ribbon. Lace the shoe, wrapping the ribbon completely around each button as you lace; tie a bow. Repeat for second shoe. Tie remaining ribbon into a bow around TuTu's neck; trim the ends.

Figure D

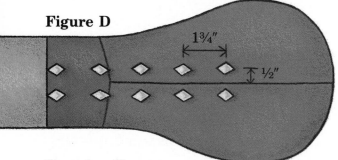

Dressing Tango

1. Cut two 13″ x 18″ pieces from yellow (pants) and two 4″ x 12″ strips from yellow stripe (pant straps).

2. Turn one pant piece right side up with 18″ edges at top and bottom. On bottom edge, locate center and draw a 4½″ line perpendicular to edge. With right sides together, sew pant pieces together only at inseam, stitching as shown. (Figure E.)
   On one pant piece, draw a 2½″ horizontal line above seam. (Figure E.) Set machine for buttonhole stitch and sew a buttonhole around line; make a slit be-

Figure E

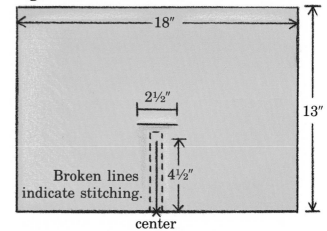

tween rows of stitching for tail. Sew side seams and press open. To hem legs, turn and press bottom edges ⅜″ and then ½″ to wrong side; machine-stitch.
   To make casing for elastic, turn and press top edge of pants ¼″ and then ⅝″ to wrong side; machine-stitch, leaving a 1½″ opening. Thread the 19″ piece of elastic through the casing. Overlap ends of elastic ½″ and zigzag-stitch together. Slip-stitch opening closed. Turn pants and place on Tango.

3. To make straps, follow first part of step 4 for TuTu. For each strap, cut a piece of ribbon same length as strap and sew ribbon to it, ¼″ from outer edge. Position a button near one end of strap; sew the button and strap to outside of pants front, slightly angling the strap. Repeat on pants back. Tie remaining piece of ribbon into a bow around Tango's neck; trim the ends.

4. For chest heart, repeat step 5 for TuTu.

5. Starting just below leg/shoe top seam, sew three buttons to one shoe, placing the buttons ½″ from center front seam and 1¾″ from each other. Repeat on other side of shoe front seam. Sew one button to center front of shoe, 3″ below last pair of buttons. Lace the shoe, wrapping the shoestring completely around each button as you lace; tie a bow. Repeat for second shoe.

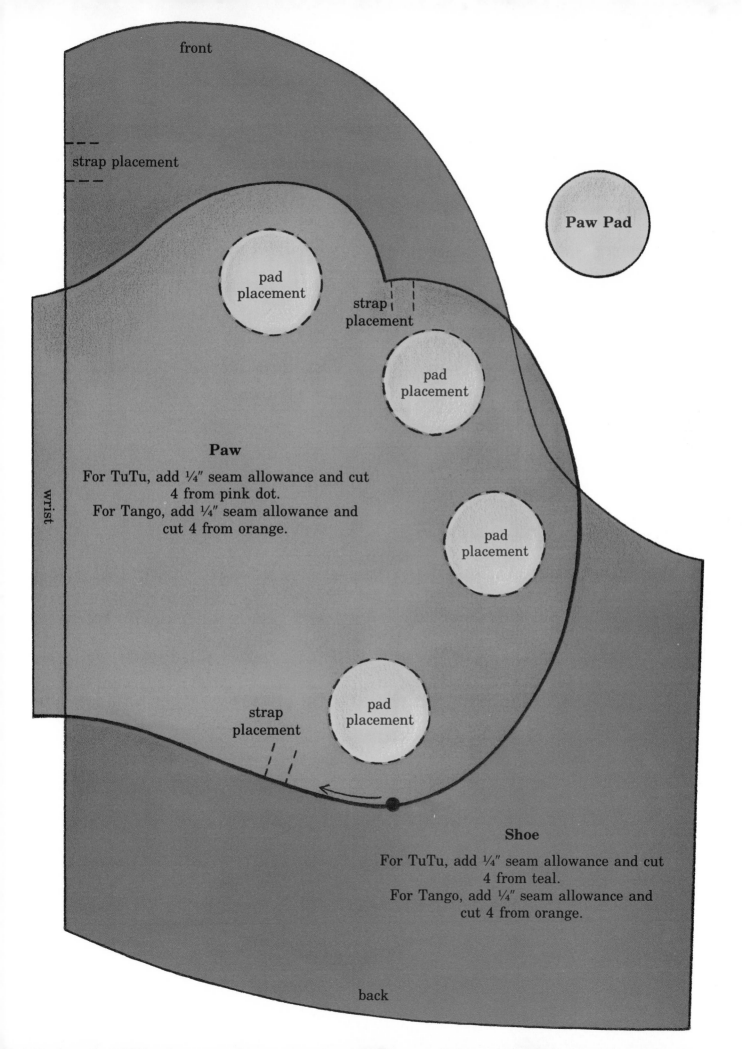

front

strap placement

Paw Pad

pad placement

strap placement

pad placement

wrist

Paw

For TuTu, add ¼″ seam allowance and cut
4 from pink dot.
For Tango, add ¼″ seam allowance and
cut 4 from orange.

pad placement

strap placement

pad placement

Shoe

For TuTu, add ¼″ seam allowance and cut
4 from teal.
For Tango, add ¼″ seam allowance and
cut 4 from orange.

back

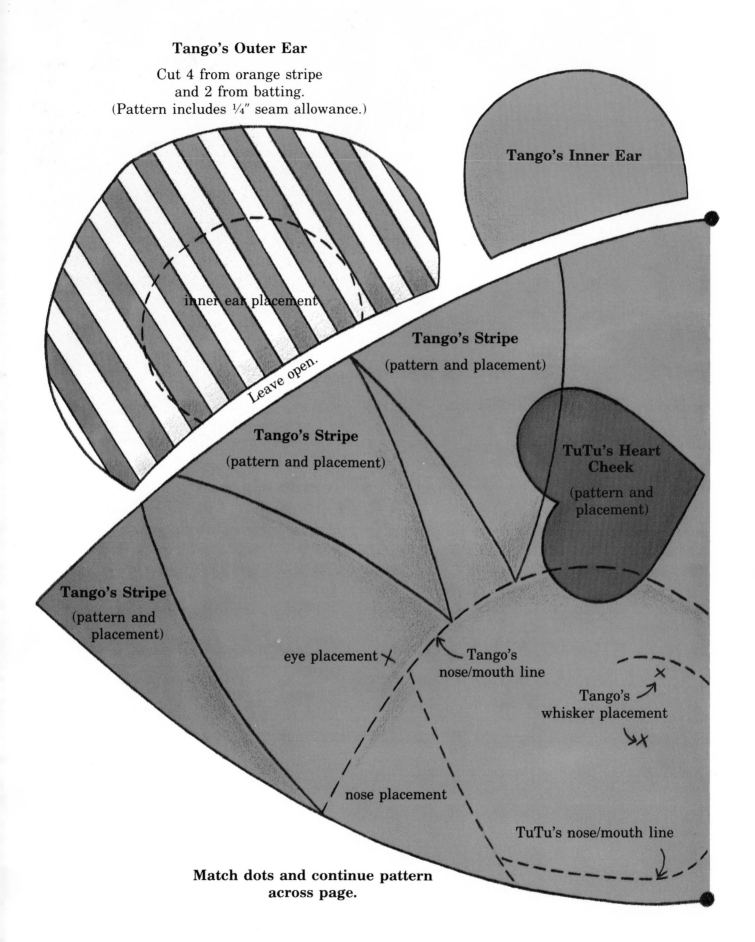

Tango's Outer Ear

Cut 4 from orange stripe
and 2 from batting.
(Pattern includes ¼″ seam allowance.)

inner ear placement

Leave open.

Tango's Inner Ear

Tango's Stripe

(pattern and placement)

Tango's Stripe

(pattern and placement)

TuTu's Heart Cheek

(pattern and placement)

Tango's Stripe

(pattern and placement)

eye placement ✗

Tango's
nose/mouth line

Tango's
whisker placement

nose placement

TuTu's nose/mouth line

**Match dots and continue pattern
across page.**

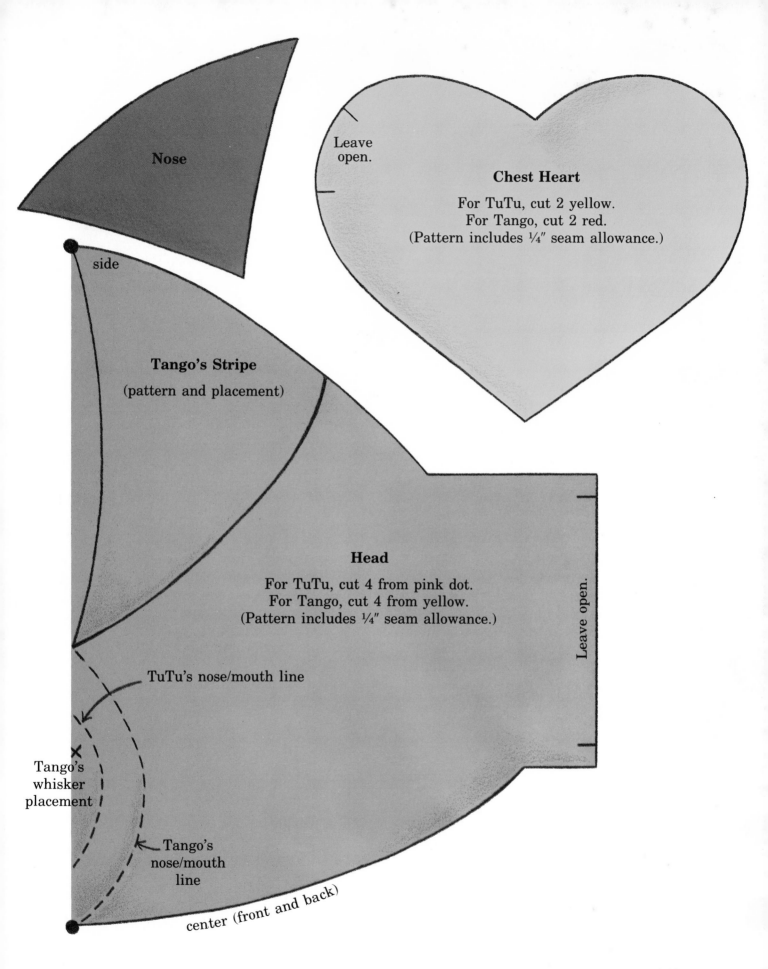

Nose

Chest Heart

For TuTu, cut 2 yellow.
For Tango, cut 2 red.
(Pattern includes ¼″ seam allowance.)

Leave open.

side

Tango's Stripe

(pattern and placement)

Head

For TuTu, cut 4 from pink dot.
For Tango, cut 4 from yellow.
(Pattern includes ¼″ seam allowance.)

Leave open.

TuTu's nose/mouth line

Tango's
whisker
placement

Tango's
nose/mouth
line

center (front and back)

Designers & Contributors

Marina Anderson, Dinosuit, 86; A-Door-a-Bells, 96; Kitty Caddy, 106.

Michel Bernstein for Michel & Co., Cross-Stitched Cowboy, 112.

Peyton Carmichael, Dip-and-Drape Angel, 30; Paperdoll Screen, 114.

Sharon A. Christman, Paper Reindeer, 38; One-of-a-Kind Cards, 52.

Barbara Griffin Forman, Buttons 'n Beads Jewelry, 66; Snowy Day Appliqué, 72; Super Socks, 77; Holiday Sweater, 85.

Connie Formby, costumes for Costume Caroling Party, 8-9; Santa hats, beards, invitation, sack, 14-17, and favor, 19, for Santa's Workshop Party.

Dot Formby, bird treats for For-the-Birds Party, 10-11.

Joyce M. Gillis, Holiday Fun Folder, 123.

Miriam C. Gourley, Away in a Manger, 42; Oatmeal Babies Necklace, 132.

Memory E. Hagler, Knit Picks, 91.

Linda Hendrickson, Merry Mice, 22; Angel Wrap, 49; Car Wash Kit, 58; Tip-Toppers, 61; Froggie Bank, 64; Mini-Mouse Scarf Set, 74; Sunny Bunnies Sweatshirt, 80; Moon Bunnies Quilt, 100; Push Chick, 120; TuTu and Tango, 134.

Zuelia Ann Hurt, Honeybear Purse, 126.

Lee Nix, Stocking Wrap, 56.

Trés Rush, Wee Weavings, 25.

Walter M. Rush, Jr., construction of Paperdoll Screen, 114.

Carol M. Tipton, Stickum-Ups, 68.

Vanessa-Ann Collection, charting of Cross-Stitched Cowboy, 112.

Madeline O'Brien White, Soapbox Soldier, 34.

Special thanks to the following shops in Birmingham, Alabama, for sharing their resources: **Applause Dancewear & Accessories; Bair's Ski & Tennis; Benetton/Brookwood; Benetton/Riverchase Galleria; Chocolate Soup, Inc.; Heirloom Shop; The Holly Tree, Inc.; Jack N' Jill Shop; Kiddieland; New Environs, Inc.; Playfair, Inc.; Ray's Children's Shop; Sikes Children's Shoes; Smith's Variety of Mountain Brook.**